BECOMING AGILE

Jossey-Bass Short Format Series

Written by thought leaders and experts in their fields, pieces in the Jossey-Bass Short Format Series provide busy, on-the-go professionals, managers, and leaders around the world with must-have, just-in-time information in a concise and actionable format.

To learn more, visit www.josseybass.com/go/shortform.

Also by the Authors

Built to Change by Edward E. Lawler, III, Christopher G. Worley, and Jerry Porras

Management Reset by Edward E. Lawler, III, Christopher G. Worley, and David Creelman

The Agility Factor: Building Adaptable Organizations for Superior Performance by Christopher G. Worley, Thomas Williams, and Edward E. Lawler, III

Assessing Organization Agility by Christopher G. Worley, Thomas Williams, and Edward E. Lawler, III

BECOMING AGILE

How the SEAM Approach to Management Builds Adaptability

CHRISTOPHER G. WORLEY
VÉRONIQUE ZARDET
MARC BONNET
AMANDINE SAVALL

JB JOSSEY-BASS™
A Wiley Brand

Published by John Wiley & Sons, Inc., Hoboken, New Jersey

Published simultaneously in Canada

For general information about our other products and services, please contact our Customer Care Department within the United States at (800) 762-2974, outside the United States at (317) 572-3993 or fax (317) 572-4002.

Wiley publishes in a variety of print and electronic formats and by print-on-demand. Some material included with standard print versions of this book may not be included in e-books or in print-on-demand. If this book refers to media such as a CD or DVD that is not included in the version you purchased, you may download this material at http://booksupport.wiley.com. For more information about Wiley products, visit www.wiley.com.

Library of Congress Cataloging-in-Publication Data

Worley, Christopher G.
Becoming agile : how the SEAM approach to management builds adaptability / Christopher G. Worley, Veronique Zardet, Marc Bonnet, Amandine Savall.
  pages cm. — (Jossey-Bass short format series)
  Includes index.
  ISBN 978-1-119-01166-8 (cloth); ISBN 978-1-119-01168-2 (pdf); ISBN 978-1-119-01167-5 (epub)
  1. Organizational change. 2. Organizational effectiveness. 3. Management. I. Title.
HD58.8.W6834 2015
658.4'06—dc23
2015020881

Printed in the United States of America
10 9 8 7 6 5 4 3 2 1

Contents

Foreword

The main challenge companies will face in the future is an issue of great importance to me. It is also a priority for Brioche Pasquier's human resource development strategy: the balance paradigm. Balance results from a reasoned consideration of the external environment versus the internal environment. The external environment demands immediacy, hyper-specialization, and a technical approach to the fields of sales management, finance, production, and other functions, but it also discourages a more holistic approach that would pay significant attention to the people in the company. To enable such a balance in organizational practices, one between the external and the internal environments, leaders must formalize a strategy, write it down, and translate it into company projects that match and reflect their being and will and draw on the company's basic management principles. Such formality helps to avoid unwarranted turnarounds that might result from unstable, turbulent, and short-term business pressures. Indeed, our aim is to sustain our strategic view over the long run.

Teamwork is the key to enabling this holistic and balanced approach. It preserves everyone's functional skills and areas of expertise. Indeed, the external pressure for hyper-specialization results in a workforce more interested in achieving personal goals and furthering their own skills and expertise at the expense of the organization's purpose. Teamwork balances this natural pressure.

Because we run a family business, we profit from our sustainability and continuity at the managerial level—and even more in regard to ownership. Our primary goal is long-term effectiveness; it is not to cope with immediacy and exogenous disruptions stemming from the external environment. Again, balancing requires fine-tuning between long-term sustainability and short-term reactions to avoid being deaf and blind to the external environment.

I'm also convinced that we have to draw on a "glocal" paradigm—thinking both globally and locally. In fact, globalization and a regional focus are not a contradiction at all. The ability to balance global and local issues is as important to tomorrow's success as the balancing of external and internal demands. Even global aspirations require local actions to take into account strategic domains, our customers and consumers, our partners, and our suppliers so that our teams can operate successfully.

The Brioche Pasquier Group chose the socio-economic approach to management (SEAM) in 1984 because our objective, since our founding in 1974, has been to remain focused on our village while also being open to the outside. Little did we know at the time, but we had already figured out how to scale the company through a "glocal" approach. From the beginning, we wanted to become a national player, but above all, to produce as close as possible to the consumers and reinforce the closeness between managers and employees within the company. Partnering with ISEOR has helped us implement and formalize organizational structures, to spread the SEAM process throughout the company. Thinking about it and being convinced of its accuracy were not sufficient. In-depth implementation was also key.

The SEAM approach taught us that a step-by-step strategy, rather than an urgent and furious one, enabled more effective, ultimately faster, and more differentiated growth and internationalization. This capability forced us to distinguish between clear objectives and the careful planning of cooperative implementation activities that best addressed the necessary changes. Such an approach and process facilitated our change management strategy, contributed to our agility, and resulted in a genuine Brioche Pasquier DNA or identity.

The socio-economic management tools that we have been practicing for more than thirty years have supported a disciplined and sustained implementation of our management principles. SEAM demands discipline and sustainable, integrated work, not "one shot" practices. The periodically negotiable activity contracts, which we call CAPs in the company (Contrats d'Amélioration Pasquier), go beyond the usual quantitative objectives, such as meeting budget, raising market share, reducing waste, or increasing productivity. In each and every CAP, managers propose quantified and tangible objectives as well as intangible objectives, such as the creation of potential. The latter are as important as the former: they consist of objectives that mentor new employees, clarify dysfunctions observed by teams in the factories, or encourage employees to improve their professional skills and teamwork on various projects. For me, those CAP objectives are the real lever to achieve the objectives of economic performance and the traditional quantified objectives. Indeed, one cannot become a production director or a sales director within a few months. It takes several semesters of hard work.

A final point about the SEAM approach is that it connects and integrates management tools together; independent, stand-alone management tools are inefficient. Articulating business plans, CAPs, and piloting logbooks really create added value that steer the company. At the Brioche Pasquier Group, we don't separate the business plan, human resource development, product development, and technical three-year projections from the six-month CAP processes that generate actions to be achieved and managerial meetings to set up. Misinterpreting such an understanding and integration would result in stacking up multiple layers of management tools and structures that would not make sense.

The book submitted by Chris Worley, Véronique Zardet, Marc Bonnet, and Amandine Savall holds up a mirror to our company. The daily immersion in the strategic piloting of a company can result in forgetting its strong points and weaknesses. When I received the manuscript, I asked a recently recruited, young, English-speaking employee to read it. She told me that the history, the strategy, and the functioning of Brioche Pasquier Group, as presented in the book, clearly reflect the current situation of the company, while shedding light on the understanding of the origins of our values and management principles.

The agility concept proposed in the book sounds relevant to me, because it shows the company's strategic journey, including the challenges we faced in Italy and Spain, and in the creation of the Pastry business unit. It also demonstrates the contribution of the analysis of dysfunctions and the work we did to learn from these challenges. The distinctive added value of the book is that it brings to light the power of SEAM. I'm much more aware of this phenomenon than ten or twenty years ago, because this methodology enhances a company's agility, as we could experience it at the Brioche Pasquier Group.

Pascal Pasquier, CEO
Brioche Pasquier Group

Preface

The book in your hand, *Becoming Agile*, is the third in a trilogy dedicated to helping executives and change practitioners understand the elements and dynamics of organization agility. *Assessing Organization Agility* summarized our perspective on agility and provided a simple but powerful tool for diagnosing a system's agile routines. In *The Agility Factor*, we described the agility framework. *The Agility Pyramid* was the result of a seven-year research program, and the book provided a variety of cases that demonstrated this dynamic capability.

This book illustrates how organization agility can be implemented using the socio-economic approach to management (SEAM) developed by the researchers at the Institute for Socio-Economic Organization Research (ISEOR). The case study presented in this book compares the principles of organization agility developed at the University of Southern California's Center for Effective Organizations with a long-term experiment supervised by Henri Savall over the past three decades. Such a long period of intervention-research in the same company beats the previous record for longitudinal participative observation held by Eliott Jaques and the Glacier Metal Company.

Henri Savall created the SEAM approach in 1973 and founded the ISEOR research center in 1975 to create a body of intervention-based knowledge using what he called the "qualimetrics research method." It is an approach aimed at observing the complexity of organization life through a variety of transformation processes. For more than forty years, Henri has trained more than 600 researchers at the ISEOR research center through intervention-research projects he conducted himself and supervised in numerous companies and organizations (1,850 so far). His ongoing and renewable energy to develop an organization's agility, as well as to manage junior and senior researchers at ISEOR, who strived to create and publish genuine, actionable, and innovative management knowledge that affect company practices, is rare.

Since 1984, the ISEOR team has experienced an outstanding partnership with the Brioche Pasquier Group and its top leaders. They have an exceptional and bold strategic vision of their family business, as well as the skills to adapt the SEAM approach to their company's setting. This publication would not have existed without Henri Savall and the Brioche Pasquier group.

Acknowledgments

Bringing this book to market has been a central endeavor of a number of colleagues and supporters who deserve recognition.

Chris' colleagues at the Center for Effective Organizations, Ed Lawler, Sue Mohrman, Gerry Ledford, John Boudreau, Alec Levenson, and Theresa Welbourne, have each contributed to this work. Ed and Sue, in particular, have been constant companions, critics, and cheerleaders; they have pushed me to think hard about how to keep this work rigorous and relevant. Alice Mark, Aaron Griffiths, and the CEO staff have also made my work meaningful with their efficient, high-quality support and their positive, energetic personalities. Everyone should be blessed with such a support network.

I've also been blessed with a thought partner who thinks hard and clear, develops insights with discipline, and brings deep experience to the work. I met Tom Williams through Jim O'Toole and Steve Wheeler, and much of this program's success is because of Tom's devotion and contribution.

As always, my family is forever. Anybody who knows me knows I am mad in love with my wife, Debbie, and our "kids," Sarah, Hannah, and Sam. For those of you who don't know me, if I'm any good at all at the things I do, it's because of my family. The best decision I've ever made was more than thirty-two years ago when I said "yes" to a relationship with Debbie. Since then, through the ups and downs of family life, my amazement at her capacity for caring, support, tolerance, and unconditional love for "a wretch like me" has grown. Deb and I are blessed to have raised three college graduates of enormous potential, and we are excited to see what paths they will choose for themselves. For now, I'm just grateful for their love and support as Dad "does his thing." To the four of you, all my love, always.

In this book, a group of long-time colleagues were able to join the research program. Through my work at Pepperdine University, the Center for Effective Organizations, and now at the NEOMA business school, I have had the privilege of working with and learning about the research at ISEOR. During my sabbatical year in Lyon, France, conversations with Marc Bonnet about organization agility and ISEOR's work with Brioche Pasquier led to visits to the organization and eventually to a decision to write this book. I am grateful to Marc (and his wife, Françoise) for making Debbie and me feel welcome in their beautiful city. Marc and Véronique Zardet made the insightful suggestion to bring Amandine Savall aboard. Amandine's doctoral dissertation into the globalization of Brioche Pasquier added critical and complementary nuance to the story.

First and foremost, Véronique thanks Henri Savall and all the ISEOR team members who have supported and facilitated this book, in particular our colleagues, Olivier Voyant, professor of management at IAE Lyon, and Frantz Datry, who are both intervention-research project leaders at ISEOR. She would also like to extend a special thank you to Serge and Louis-Marie Pasquier, the company leaders in 1984, and to

Pascal, who has been CEO since 2007. He is steering an ambitious internationalization strategy through managerial agility.

Many thanks to Chris Worley, who proposed challenging and stimulating interactions that enabled the publication of this book; Marc and Amandine, who supported Véronique in this fabulous project. It was a six-month team experience that supplemented all of the team's skills and backgrounds. Indeed, it was a truly international process!

This book wouldn't exist without the opportunity afforded by meeting with our North American colleagues, who became friends and have strongly supported ISEOR since 1998. They have facilitated its publications and the dissemination of SEAM in North America: thank you to David Boje and Grace Anne Rosile, Anthony Buono, Peter Sorensen and Therese Yaeger, Murray Lindsay, Robert Gephart, John Conbere and Alla Heoriadi, not to mention all those we have met since then.

Véronique thanks her family, her parents, and her daughters and their husbands as well as the grandchildren who have supported her for more than thirty years, particularly during the tense moments focused on preparing a book to be released.

For Marc, this book is a tribute to those who proved to be agile and tenacious enough to spur innovation in the field of management science. Indeed, Henri Savall supervised this intervention-research project for over three decades, a research process that is unique in our field. From the very beginning, Brioche Pasquier's leaders have been daring and have embedded the values of human potential development in a structured way through ISEOR's socio-economic approach to management (SEAM). Together, the leaders, company managers, and employees are the very embodiment of managerial nimbleness.

Amandine's first acknowledgments are for her three co-authors, who invited her to be part of this fabulous project. It is a huge honor for her that Chris Worley agreed to be part of her Ph.D. committee in December 2014, despite the distance. Their collaboration around her dissertation and this book is a proud achievement. She also acknowledges Véronique Zardet and Henri Savall. Their rigor, organization, ethics, and entrepreneurship energize her every day. She thanks them also for hiring her at ISEOR, where she learned about intervention-research and Brioche Pasquier. They are and will be examples to be followed. Finally, she would like to thank Professor Marc Bonnet, the third co-author, who helped her network with many wonderful scholars in the United States, particularly Chris Worley.

I would like to thank my SEAM mentor, Frantz Datry. A special thought to him for teaching me about intervention-research techniques. He supported me through the process of writing this book. To Professor Michel Péron, thank you for reading, editing, advising, and supporting me in my English publications.

Another fabulous acquaintance was with Brioche Pasquier. First, I thank Pascal Pasquier, CEO, for trusting me and opening the doors of his company. His simplicity, modesty, and professionalism made our discussions even more memorable. I would like to thank Fabrice Sciumbata (international director), Jean-François Boissinot (Toasted Bread BU director), and Valérie Girard (export manager), as well as all their international teams, for their wholehearted cooperation in carrying out the field research and insights described in Chapter 3. A special word of thanks to the directors of the subsidiaries and their teams for their warm welcome: Paul Levitan and Jean-Yves Charron (in Richmond, California),

Pablo Ocariz and Alberto Susaño (in Irún, Spain), and Olivier Ripoche (in Milton Keynes, UK).

Professor Anthony Buono is a dear friend of Amandine's family. The way he considers research and his warm welcoming at the Management Consulting Division of the Academy of Management helped me to succeed in my doctoral research. I would like to acknowledge my admiration to the big family of scholars-practitioners in the field of organization development and change led by Peter Sorensen and Therese Yaeger from Benedictine University in Chicago. Thanks to Professors Robert Gephart and Murray Lindsay, whose work and path in management sciences inspired me in understanding different parts of organizational agility.

Last but not least, thanks go to my husband Cédric Anago, who has always accepted my professional career and the time I've devoted to it.

Finally, all of us would like to thank the editors and staff at Jossey-Bass/Wiley. Kathe Sweeney was and is a long-time supporter of the work at the Center for Effective Organizations. Alison Hankey kept us focused on the manuscript, and we are grateful for Jeanenne Ray's continuity and "let's get it done" attitude. The copy editing and production teams, as always, have done a great and efficient job of putting this through the process.

Christopher G. Worley, Reims, France

Véronique Zardet, Lyon, France

Marc Bonnet, Lyon, France

Amandine Savall, Lyon, France

1

One Vision, Two Perspectives

Agility and the Socio-Economic Organization

For JCDecaux, the Paris initiative was much more complex than the Lyon project.*

Back in 2005, in another of a long string of game-changing innovations, the leading outdoor advertising agency had implemented a bicycle management system that made bikes

---

*Data for the JCDecaux case was drawn from several sources, including JCDecaux. Reference Document. Retrieved from www.jcdecaux.com/en/content/search?SearchText=2013+Reference+document&x=0&y=0,; P. Coles, E. Corsi, and V. Dessain. (2012). "On two wheels in Paris: The Velib bicycle sharing program," Cambridge, MA: Harvard Business School Press; K. Schweizer. (2013). "French advertiser JCDecaux begins US push with Chicago billboards," retrieved from www.businessweek.com/articles/2013-05-30/french-advertiser-jcdecaux-begins-u-dot-s-dot-push-with-chicago-billboards.

available to people in Lyon's city center. Local citizens and tourists signed up through an online system, picked up bikes with their passwords at various stations around the city, and returned the bikes to the same or a different station for little or no money. This system relieved traffic congestion, improved air quality, increased foot traffic for local merchants, and generated revenue for both the city and JCDecaux (JCD). Similar systems had been piloted in Amsterdam, Vienna, and elsewhere, but Lyon was one of the first such systems implemented on a large scale.

In exchange for setting up, managing, and maintaining the system, JCD could sell the space on billboards, bus stop stations, and other "street furniture" in the city. It was a business model developed by Jean-Claude Decaux in the early 1970s, and Lyon had been the first city to sign up for the concept. Lyon's success with the initial program extended over the years to tram stops, airport kiosks, and, when the city wanted to reduce its carbon footprint, JCDecaux had a solution. The VéloV program was a big success.

Where Lyon had about 3,700 bikes, the Paris system, originally launched on July 15, 2007, with 10,000 bikes and 750 rental stations, quickly grew to 20,600 bikes and 1,450 stations in two years. The ten-year license for 1,628 billboards around the city, and the right to convert them into modern, moving billboards that could rotate among three advertisers, allowed Paris to receive all the revenues from the bike rentals. JCD could recoup up to 12 percent of bike rental revenues if the program met six quality standards. The city designed the bikes and chose the placement of stations, but JCD was responsible for all other obligations, including maintenance. JCDecaux would pay the city a €2 million annual royalty with a €15 million bonus over the ten years.

Similar to the Lyon system, the Vélib' system—a contraction of Vélo (bike) and liberté (liberty)—allowed anyone to subscribe for €1/day, €5/week, or €29/year. The first half-hour of any use was free and, after that, a low fee was applied. The system opened on time and with the right numbers. By the end of the first year, there were nearly 200,000 annual subscribers, 100,000 users/day, and over twenty-seven million rentals. Each bike had an electronic tracking system to help balance supply and deter theft. In addition, the system was very "green" and reflected JCD's commitment to high quality and service. JCD employees regularly washed all bikes and stations with recovered rainwater and no detergent. Bicycles were made with recycled materials, and stations operated under an electricity contract that used energy only when the solar panels could not provide the required power. The initial results were so promising that Paris officials wanted JCD to extend the Vélib' program to thirty suburban municipalities.

But all was not rosy. Despite the tracking system, there were high levels of theft and vandalism. According to a June 2009 estimate, 8,000 of the 20,000 bicycles had disappeared and 18,000 bikes had been vandalized. The cost increases made the operating model unsustainable and JCDecaux wanted to renegotiate quality metrics and cost-sharing agreements. In addition to the theft and vandalism issues, JCD quickly learned that the quality standards had been set too high. The Paris system was so large and the population so diverse that the performance objectives had amounted to educated guesses. City officials agreed and reopened contract negotiations.

In July 2008, Paris paid JCD €7 million/year for the extension of Vélib's program and would reimburse JCD €400/stolen bike beyond the first 4 percent of the fleet and up to 25 percent. In January 2009, a third round of negotiations took place. The city paid JCD €2.6 million to increase call center employees and changed JCD's incentives to increase the number of subscribers.

Even with all the adjustments and payments, co-CEO Jean-Francois Decaux noted that, from the beginning, the bicycle program had not cost the city a single euro. In fact, both sides were making money with Vélib'. The city was getting free public infrastructure and ongoing maintenance and JCD had a stable source of advertising space revenue. The business model was evolving along the same lines of other street furniture initiatives.

Purpose of the Book

The case of JCDecaux in Paris—in fact, the organization's history in France and worldwide—demonstrates an advanced organization capability in practice. We call this capability "agility"—the ability to make *timely, effective, and sustained* organization changes when changing circumstances require it (Worley, Williams, & Lawler, 2014). Agility, and the implementation processes necessary to become adaptable, is the subject of this book. This chapter introduces our objectives and purposes and briefly describes the two frameworks, agility and the socio-economic theory of organizations, explored and integrated in this book.

JCDecaux's successful implementation of the biking systems in Lyon and Paris is a reflection of the organization's broader agility. Agile organizations can make *timely* changes because they are better able to perceive short- and long-term environmental demands. JCDecaux demonstrated an outstanding ability to perceive changes in its environment, an ability that has been developed and reinforced over time through its organization structure, communication systems, and human resource management practices. Fully 65 percent of JCD's employees work in field operations where they are close to the customer and the public they serve. They are installing and maintaining all kinds of street furniture and trading out advertisements on a daily, weekly, and monthly basis. They notice what others see—broken advertising displays, changes in the neighborhood, or missing bikes—and report on these issues using mobile applications.

When bicycles in Paris were being vandalized and stolen at proportions that far exceeding typical rates, that information was transmitted to decision-makers. When stations were completely empty or completely full such that customers could not take or could not leave bikes, the tracking system fed that information to the operations center, where crews could be dispatched to re-distribute bikes as necessary. All that data rolled up to decision-makers, who could compare existing operations against contractual obligations, assess the level of performance, and signal the need for operational adjustments or the need to revisit terms of the agreement. Moreover, a strong system of on-boarding and training new employees, a reward system that incented people to care about quality and performance, and a policy of hiring full-time over part-time employees to engender commitment to quality helped to support that expectation of communication.

On a broader scale, JCD's sales and marketing organization is monitoring cities around the world for upcoming contract expirations or renewal opportunities, working with design firms on the latest and most efficient street furniture concepts, and strategizing how to win against an increasingly concentrated set of competitors. For example, in anticipation of the New York City contract, JCDecaux worked to understand the city's objectives, problems, and challenges. Two years before the existing contract was to expire, they offered to place and maintain a set of self-cleaning toilets throughout the city to see whether urinating in public could be reduced. Activities like these helped JCD make timely changes.

Agile organizations make *effective* changes because their members understand and share a commitment to the strategy. This shared understanding and commitment helps people to know what changes are most important to execution. JCD is guided by a commitment to innovation and quality. Their aggressive pursuit of quality and innovation differentiates JCD in their chosen advertising segment on a global basis.

The Lyon, New York, and Paris stories demonstrate that JCD has no problem trying things out and implementing the things that work. A long stream of innovation in related areas also shows that they are able to learn and to apply those learnings to organization changes and proactive strategies. After only a few months of operations in Paris, by far the largest system implemented at that time, the organization had learned that the quality standards established in the initial contract were unobtainable and worked with Paris officials to find a win-win solution. JCD thus demonstrated the ability to change along two dimensions. Their innovations in outdoor advertising, street furniture, transportation/airports, and billboards have produced a number of product and service changes and confirm the ability to adapt. In addition, their flexibility in Paris, and its similarity to other product life cycles, demonstrates the ability to adjust quickly. Having a clear and shared strategy as well as the ability and willingness to experiment and implement changes allow agile organizations to make effective changes.

Finally, agile organizations make *sustained* changes. As discussed above, JCD not only implemented change, but those changes were allowed to operate as long as they were contributing to improved performance. If they were not, JCD did not wring their hands over sunk costs and stick to "the way things have always been done." When a system stopped working, it was eligible for change. Allowing changes to operate—but not become institutionalized—helps agile organizations make sustained change.

In today's economy, the need for a flexible organization capable of initiating and responding to change well is clear, but stories like JCDecaux's are rare. By our own and others' estimates, less than 18 percent of large, public firms are able to design and operate the strategies and organizations that can change effectively enough to sustain above average levels of performance over long periods of time (McGahan, 1999a, b; Worley, Williams, & Lawler, 2014). JCD has been doing it since 1974.

In the United States and Europe, there is a lot of rhetoric about being nimble and agile. There is research and practice to support agile software development, adaptive leadership, and flexible manufacturing. But there is little work on what it means to be an agile organization, how it is designed and operated, and any performance advantages that might derive from it. Worse, the methods and practices of transforming organizations are ancient. Most firms rely on weak forms of an "unfreeze-move-refreeze" theory created in the 1950s or extensions of similar linear change management models (Worley & Mohrman, 2014).

The purpose of this book is to help fill that gap. It summarizes the findings from a seven-year study of organization agility conducted by the University of Southern California's Center for Effective Organizations (CEO) and extensions developed at the NEOMA Business School. It also demonstrates how agility can be implemented through the application of the socio-economic approach to management (SEAM), a change process developed by the intervention-researchers at the Institute for Socio-Economic Organization Research (ISEOR) over the past forty years.

The book compares these frameworks and demonstrates how agility and SEAM complement one another. A SEAM intervention at the French company, Brioche Pasquier, represents both an effective implementation of the agile capability and the establishment of agility as a driver of performance. Our primary conclusion is that SEAM's focus on "hidden costs" and the low performance resulting from (mostly) unintended organization design and human resource practices is an important manifestation of the lack of agility. We argue that agility requires efficiency where it matters most, whereas inefficiency (slack) is important in other areas where innovation and creativity and testing need to occur. The SEAM methodology embraces that complexity. It is not always and monolithically devoted to removing hidden costs, but encourages and supports the appropriate allocation of resources to creative tasks. For example, one of its management tools, the "periodically negotiable activity contract," invites individuals to identify and propose projects and experiments to improve the organization through the identification of human and economic potential.

Agility and Performance

The concept of agility is not new. At one time, adaptability and flexibility—two possible synonyms for agility—were the most frequently mentioned criteria for judging an organization's effectiveness (Steers, 1975). Unfortunately, the interest in adaptability—whether an organization can respond to change *over time*—as a measure of organization effectiveness waned and fragmented into functional and cross-sectional views of financial and operational performance. Strategists and executives preferred financial performance measures, operating managers looked at productivity and efficiency, human resource professionals wondered about workforce engagement and the kind of culture that was produced, and marketing managers worried about market share and brand reputation. Research approaches reflected a similar discipline-based bias and, as a result, integrated measures, such as adaptability or development, were less in vogue. Moreover, in the wake of Reagan/Thatcher era policies favoring economic deregulation and market focus, most studies of organization effectiveness debated the pros and cons of different financial measures.

Recent reviews of performance metrics suggest three broad categories: financial market, accounting, and mixed measures, such as balanced scorecards (Richard, Devinney, Yip, & Johnson, 2009). Financial market measures, such as stock price and total shareholder return (TSR), are often preferred because they are considered "objective," difficult to manipulate over anything but the very short term, reflect outside investors' perceptions of value, and have the benefit of being a single measure against which *any* public firm can be judged. However, of the 213 articles published between 2005 and 2007, only 17 percent used financial market measures, while 53 percent used accounting measures. The most commonly used measure, ROA, was used in 6 percent of the studies. TSR was the second most common measure, used in only 3 percent of the studies. There is clearly no agreed-on measure.

But as the pace of change, especially globalization, technology, regulation and deregulation, and workforce characteristics, continued to increase, executive and researcher attention has returned to an interest in agility, adaptability, and flexibility. More specifically, the interest has focused on understanding the relationship between organization change and performance. Today, there are three views of the relationship, the ecological perspective, the transformation perspective, and a dynamic capabilities/learning perspective.

The Ecological Perspective

The first view is best framed by an "ecological" or biological perspective. In the standard telling of industrial evolution, small, upstart, and nimble firms overtake large, established, successful, and mostly inert firms. They grow to look and behave like their victims, and the cycle repeats. Microsoft's emergence dislodged many of the high-tech firms in the emerging computer and software industry. Today, many investors and executives wonder whether the latest round of start-ups will eventually displace Microsoft.

This school of thought proposes that a merciless Darwinian world exists in which, industry by industry, new organizations are born and old ones incapable of changing die off, resulting in a new population of organizations. The Schumpeterian forces of change are the same as those in biological ecosystems: variation, selection, and retention, and the basic measure of performance is survival. That is, organization change is not defined by how a single organization becomes different but by the differences in the characteristics of a group (that is, an industry) of organizations. In Figure 1.1, only Firms A and F survive over time, and organization change is described by differences among the six firms at time t and the four firms at time t+1.

Clayton Christensen demonstrated this dynamic in *The Innovator's Dilemma* (Christensen, 1997). Richard D'Aveni (1994) also captured this idea in his concept of "hypercompetition"—

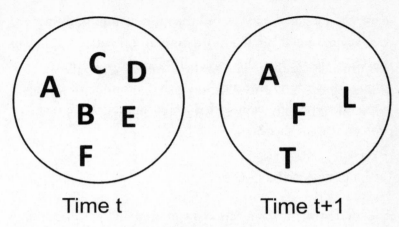

Time t   Time t+1

Figure 1.1   The Ecological Perspective

competitive conditions so turbulent and uncertain that competitive advantages and profits resulting from them cannot be
sustained. In fact, recent research has found that market environments have become increasingly turbulent over the past
decade, and that the persistence of competitive advantage and
sustained performance has gotten shorter (D'Aveni, Dagnino,
& Smith, 2010).

According to the ecological perspective, the environment determines whether large firms are better than small
firms, global firms more fit than domestic firms, or diversified
firms are selected over single-product firms. Organizations
can try to change through variations, such as reorganizations,
financial restructurings, layoffs/downsizing, innovation, and
growth. However, organizational inertia—the inability to
change at a rate at least equal to environmental change—is
the result of commitments to courses of action that constrain
responses. For example, movie and music entertainment
companies seemed completely surprised by the emergence
of the Internet and other digital technologies, responded
too late, and did so inappropriately. The more organizations

grow, the longer they live, and the more committed they are to a way of operating, the more inert and resistant to change they become. When the forces of "natural selection" come calling, they are so overwhelming that attempts to change a company to realign its fit with the environment have very low probabilities of success.

The Transformation Perspective

A second view of organization adaptation and performance is captured by the transformation model. This perspective argues that the inertial forces described by the ecological perspective are real, but that organizations need to change rarely to survive and thrive. Measures of performance are extended from binary notions of life or death to financial and accounting indicators of organization effectiveness. Organization change and performance follow similar but mirrored patterns, as shown in Figure 1.2.

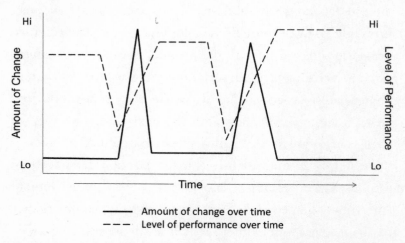

——— Amount of change over time
– – – Level of performance over time

Figure 1.2 The Transformational Perspective

Over *relatively* long time periods, the amount of organization change is low and focused on incremental efforts in support of a particular strategy and organization design that yields high levels of performance. When environments change, the organization's existing offerings and operations become misaligned with the new demands. Performance drops, quickly or slowly, and eventually forces the organization into transformation— a relatively short period of revolutionary organization change along multiple dimensions, including strategy, structure, management processes, and HR practices.

Unaccustomed to these disruptions, firms often adopt reactive change management practices that set new objectives and develop new practices intended to move the organization from its current state to a future one that is, one hopes, more aligned with environmental demands. Research and experience suggest that, when these transformations are conducted quickly and effectively, often with the help of outside consultants, they ensure survival, set the organization on another steady path of low organization change, and return the organization to profitability (Lant & Mezias, 1992; Romanelli & Tushman, 1994). IBM's transformation from computer manufacturer to services provider is one of the best-known examples. However, research also suggests that few of these transformations deliver their anticipated results. The relative length of high or low performance depends on the organization's ability to conduct timely and effective transformations.

An important bridge between the ecological/transformational views and the third perspective is the way environmental change is conceived. The first two perspectives characterize environmental change as discontinuous. Technology, regulation, and social expectations change relatively slowly over long periods of time until they are interrupted by relatively short periods of dramatic change (Tushman & Anderson, 1986). Under these conditions, organization adaptation could mimic the environment (as in the transformational view) or could be ruled by the forces of variation, selection, and retention (as in the ecological view). The third view conceives of environmental change as more continuously disruptive. A 2014 study by the HR firm i4cp found that more than 64 percent of companies reported experiencing a disruption in their environment within the past twenty-four months (i4cp.com, 2014).

The Dynamic Capabilities/Learning Perspective

The third view is best framed by the "dynamic capabilities" or "organization learning" school. While acknowledging that organization inertia can exist, this argument suggests that the capability to change resources and processes repeatedly can result in consistent performance. Like environmental change, organization change in this model is relatively constant. Organizations can have strategies, structures, resources, processes, and routines that allow them to both sense and adapt to environmental threats and opportunities as well as intentionally execute on strategic initiatives. These dynamic capabilities deliver appropriate organization changes when and where they are needed. Rather than adhere to a particular set of management practices expected to serve them well under any and all circumstances, firms with healthy dynamic capabilities build (and drop) a variety of "ordinary" capabilities, possess organization structures that adjust, and so on. Sometimes they "stick to the knitting," and sometimes they diversify a little; sometimes they get really close to their customers, and sometimes they distance themselves; sometimes they use "homegrown" management, and sometimes they bring in outsiders; sometimes they use participative leadership styles, and sometimes a new direction will be dictated; and sometimes, good enough is good enough. Firms with strong dynamic and learning capabilities would manifest a performance pattern different from mere survival or the intermittent drops associated with the transformational model. They would perform consistently above average (Figure 1.3).

Several researchers have tried to capture this wholistic, dynamic perspective. For example, Verlboda (1998) argued that organization flexibility required executives to embrace the paradox of stability and change, what we now call ambidexterity. He proposed that the paradox was resolved through a sophisticated and complex set of technical and structural design features that allowed the organization to unlearn old habits and be open to new opportunities.

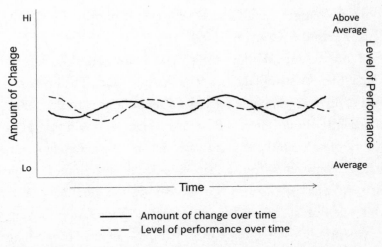

Figure 1.3 The Dynamic Capabilities Perspective

Sull (2008) suggested that organizations should (1) culti-vate capabilities that allow the organization to proactively pur-sue opportunities and (2) build stores of reserves or capability for absorbing shock and change. Haeckel (1999) argued that, despite the rhetoric, most organizations act like a closed sys-tem in pursuit of efficiency. He proposed that organizations should really adopt an open system perspective that develops the capabilities to sense external signals, and within a context of purpose, develop appropriate responses. Finally, in the UK, Pettigrew and his colleagues suggested that organization per-formance should increase with the adoption of three comple-mentary sets of organization change: (1) increased flexibility through project-based structures, flatter structures, and de-centralized decision making, (2) more permeable boundaries through a narrower focus, the outsourcing of non-core tasks, and the development of alliance capabilities, and (3) more ro-bust processes through increased horizontal communication, IT investments, and empowered HR practices. They found that increased performance was highest when organizations adopted changes in all three sets (Whittington, Pettigrew, Peck, Fenton, & Conyon, 1999).

More recently, Worley, Williams, and Lawler (2014) suggest-ed that there are two standards for assessing agility. The first stan-dard of agility is outcome related. Organizations with the ability to make timely, effective, and sustained change should have (1) a history of successful changes that result in (2) profitability rates that are consistently (more than 80 percent of the time) higher than the average of their competitive group over time. Thus, while survival is a necessary but not sufficient condition for agil-ity, it is not the same thing. Firms that have survived over a long period have clearly adapted, but that does not mean they are agile. Organization agility is manifest in a variety of organization changes that result in sustained, above-average performance.

The second standard of agility is organizational. It is important to know that an organization possesses the strategies, structures, and systems that can drive change and sustained performance. We need to know that change and performance are the result of capability, not just luck. The Agility Pyramid (Figure 1.4) describes the importance of and the relationships among agility routines, differentiated capabilities, and management practices.

The Routines of Agility

Agile firms want to be adaptable so they can change better than their competitors. At the top of the pyramid, agility represents an institutionalized ability to do different things or do

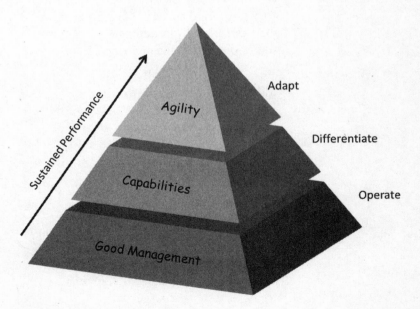

Figure 1.4 The Agility Pyramid

things differently when and where they create a performance advantage for the firm. Researchers found that four routines distinguished the high performing organizations (Table 1.1). These companies have the ability to *strategize* in dynamic ways, accurately *perceive* changes in their external environment, *test* possible responses, and *implement* changes in products, technology, operations, structures, systems, and capabilities. While these routines have their parallels in other organization theories, the hard work and expertise necessary to implement and orchestrate them in dynamic ways to produce consistent high performance is advanced and uncommon. We will explore these routines in detail throughout the book.

Table 1.1 The Routines of Agility

Routine	Description
Strategizing	How top management teams establish an aspirational *purpose*, develop a widely shared *strategy*, and manage the climate and commitment to *execution*.
Perceiving	The process of broadly, deeply, and continuously monitoring the environment to *sense* changes, rapidly *communicate* these perceptions to decision-makers who *interpret* and formulate appropriate responses.
Testing	How the organization *sets up, runs, and learns from experiments.*
Implementing	How the organization maintains its *ability and capacity to implement changes*, both incremental and discontinuous, as well as its ability to *verify the contribution of execution* to performance.

The Pivotal Role of Differentiated Capabilities

The capabilities level in the pyramid describes the source of current performance and value creation. Capabilities represent the ability and capacity of an organization to get certain things done. "Ordinary" capabilities, such as lowering costs or improving quality, allow the organization to keep pace with a changing world. Other capabilities, such as designing superior customer experiences, developing new products faster, or more efficiently gaining scale in emerging markets, are often called "differentiating" capabilities. They add value in distinct ways. Organizations that can identify, develop, and implement ways to be better, faster, or cheaper than their competitors are able to achieve better than average profitability.

However, our theory of agility parts ways with traditional perspectives at this point. Most management theories encourage organizations to preserve, protect, and defend their differentiated positions by raising switching costs, protecting intellectual property, or fine-tuning competency models to support existing operations. As a result, managers often hurry to make specific, and in some cases large and irreversible, commitments to sustain the advantage. Too many energy companies became experts at coal or nuclear power generation and are ill-prepared to make the shift to wind and solar. The cruel joke is that, in attempting to preserve the advantage, organizations can over-commit to institutionalization, becoming more inert and vulnerable to environmental shifts.

Agile firms are engaged in a dangerous game. On the one hand, they know they must develop differentiated capabilities to drive above-average performance today, but they cannot over-invest in capabilities that will not serve them in the future. The agile routines possess the power and ability to change capabilities. They keep the organization focused on the capabilities that delivery profits today while also looking out for the capabilities that will be needed in the future.

The Good Management Practices

What facilitates the effective execution of today's and tomorrow's capabilities are the management practices at the bottom of the pyramid. These familiar "good management" practices include planning, organizing, leading, and motivating an organization. Good management involves, among other things, being able to formulate a strategy and objectives, develop capital and operating budgets, and reward employees in a systematic manner. However, traditional organizations are dominated by annual budgets, annual performance appraisal systems, and merit-based pay systems. They define leadership as a level in the hierarchy. Leaders are the people who occupy senior positions. Such systems not only constrain the effectiveness of the agility routines, but they make everyday changes difficult. Innovation, experimentation, and responses to market opportunities are held hostage to an annual timetable, centralized decision making, and complaints that "it's not in the budget."

Well-managed companies often adopt best practices and institutionalize them in support of the capabilities they believe will confer a sustainable competitive advantage. They may align their performance management systems to incent execution of the current strategy, implement sophisticated six-sigma programs, and define leadership as an individual trait that is developed in mostly "high potential" managerial employees. But while these investments make the organization successful today, they also make it more difficult to change when the capabilities outlive their relevance. Change requires a jolt to the system from a new leader, a market disruption, or some other exogenous force.

What characterizes the agile organizations are management systems that are designed to operate at a faster "clock speed" and change easily, even as they deliver effectiveness. For example, goal-setting processes occur more frequently and incentive systems reward execution, change, and behaviors that align to corporate mission, purpose, and values. Agile organizations have flexible methods for allocating people, money, time, and other resources to their most important uses and balance short- and long-term horizons. As a result, agile firms define leadership as an organization capacity and view anyone in the organization as capable of influencing change.

The theory of agility described by Worley, Williams, and Lawler (2014) falls mostly under the dynamic capability and organization learning perspective. But it also draws on insights and implications from the other two approaches. Like the ecological view, their theory of agility acknowledges that organization inertia is real and addresses that by *internalizing* the variation-selection-retention forces of organizational ecology to create more flexibility. For example, agile organizations recognize the power of the external environment to both change the basis of competition and to select the firms that best address competitive requirements. As a result, they build sophisticated perceiving routines to sense environmental change and generate a variety of alternative short- and long-term scenarios as well as an appropriate number of potential solutions and responses. Building this robust set of potential strategies prepares the organization for a different number of futures and prevents the organization from becoming too comfortable with the current strategy.

Similarly, agile organizations understand the strong motivation to invest in switching costs and other mechanisms to retain successful adaptations that protect and attempt to sustain a competitive advantage. But they are not lured to adopt such practices. Agile organizations recognize that such investments are a primary contributor to inertia and can increase the risk of failure during change. Change that might be relatively easy during early stages of success becomes more difficult in later stages of success. Traditional organizations dismiss or extinguish much of the diversity in talent, knowledge, perspectives, technologies, and systems that would support new ways of operating to support a one best way of doing things. As a result, agile organizations engage in deliberate experiments (variation and selection) and leverage incentive systems that encourage both performance and change (retention).

Like the punctuated equilibrium model, agility assumes that change is possible but largely inefficient in most organizations for two reasons. First, organization change is inefficient because traditional organization design principles assume stability and reliability are the keys to performance (Katz & Kahn, 1978). As with the inertia argument above, organizations tend to respond to marketplace demands for consistency. Second, organization change is inefficient because most approaches to change are not fit to the task. Despite their focus, most change management models view change as an event that will end so that stability and reliability can be restored. Failures in organization change, therefore, are partly a function of the relatively weak forms of change management that are available to executives.

A Socio-Economic Theory of Organizations

At roughly the same time the organization theorists were arguing over models of change and effectiveness, a different conversation was taking place in France and Europe. There was deep concern that organization change in response to the turbulence of the 1970s was ineffective. In many ways, executives were managing organizations according to principles of bureaucracy and scientific management developed decades earlier. The tremendous insights and applied successes from the Tavistock Institute's socio-technical work design breakthroughs and McGregor's proposals regarding the promise and potential of human participation and involvement in organization decision making were not diffusing (McGregor, 1960; Trist & Bamforth, 1951). Organizations clung to approaches that centralized power in the hands of a few. Perrow's (1971) warning about bureaucracy's ability to concentrate power was embraced by those who could and unheeded by those who should.

The TFW Virus in Organizations

A basic assumption in the development of a socio-economic theory of organizations (Buono & Savall, 2015; Savall & Zardet, 2012) was the existence of a metaphorical virus. In a nutshell, the "TFW" (short for Taylor-Fayol-Weber) virus hinders the organizational processes required to promote performance, engagement, and adaptability. Indeed, the TFW virus results in the inability to collaborate, thwarts information sharing, sabotages management and decision-making processes, and prevents the termination or improvement of low value added tasks and processes (Savall & Zardet, 2008). It is one of the main drivers of dysfunction and poor performance in modern organizations, and so widespread and embedded in managers' mindsets that most people are unaware of its influence. The virus contains assumptions and principles of organizing that do not respond to or align with the demands of today's marketplace.

The TFW virus owes its power to three early organizational theorists, Frederick Winslow Taylor, Henri Fayol, and Max Weber, whose collective works had an enormous influence over modern management practice. Taylor is widely known for his efficiency approach to job and work design. For any particular set of tasks and activities, Taylor would study the physical motions involved and the time it took to complete them. Work designed according these "scientific" principles was highly efficient and productive, lowered training costs, and required little supervision. The remnants of this approach are easily found today in most organizations.

Although Taylor intended these scientific principles to make work safer and more productive and to make workers less prone to injury, he did not accord workers much intelligence. He once told the U.S. Congress that the pig iron process in steel making was so complex that anyone who was dumb enough to choose this type of work for an occupation could not be smart enough to understand it. The implicit but false assumption behind Taylorism was that human beings are not able to learn efficiently or utilize multiple skills effectively. As a result, the principles of task specialization and their implementation in job designs turned employees into mere instruments of production and ignored their creativity and potential.

Henri Fayol was influenced by Taylor's theories, but noted that Taylor worked from the "bottom up" to discover the most efficient way to do work. Fayol, on the other hand, was interested in how to structure the work of management. Fayol, among others, is largely credited with the creation of the specialized functional organization chart. It is generally regarded as the most utilized structure in organizations today. The functional structure derived from Fayol's principles of management that favored the division of labor into specialized units; the establishment of clear lines of authority, unity of command, and direction; the centralization of key decisions; and the stability of tenure.

The primary strengths of the functional structure include the promotion of specialization in skills and resources by grouping people who perform similar work and face similar problems. This grouping facilitates communication within departments and allows specialists to share their expertise through standardized processes. It also enhances career development within the specialty. However, functional structures tend to promote routine task behaviors with a narrow view of organizational functioning. Department members focus on their own tasks, rather than on the organization's overall value-added processes. This can lead to conflict across functional departments when each group tries to maximize its own performance without considering the performance of other units. Functional structures often result in organizational silos that make internal integration, coordination, and change difficult. Coordination and scheduling among departments, often called the "white space" problem, can be difficult when each emphasizes its own perspective.

Max Weber argued that bureaucracy was the most efficient and rational way to organize social systems and that systematic processes and organized hierarchies were necessary to maintain order, maximize efficiency, and eliminate favoritism. He stated, "from a purely technical point of view, a bureaucracy is capable of attaining the highest degree of efficiency, and is in this sense formally the most rational known means of exercising authority over human beings. It is superior to any other form in precision, in stability, in the stringency of its discipline, and in its reliability" (Rheinstein, 1968, p. 223). Weber believed the ideal bureaucracy would have a functional structure, clear lines and limits of authority over specific areas, rational decision making and action taking by neutral officials, and career advancement based on technical qualifications. To be fair, despite all of the negative connotations associated with the term, "bureaucracy" is simply an administrative system for governing large institutions. In fact, Weber feared bureaucracy might threaten individual freedom and lead to a "soulless iron cage" of trapped individuals.

Taylor, Fayol, and Weber were trying to improve the functioning of organizations. At the same time, and perhaps unintentionally, much of their work resulted in dehumanized organizations focused on maintaining the status quo. Weber, for example, stated, "The more completely [the organization] succeeds in eliminating from official business love, hatred, and all purely personal, irrational, and emotional elements which escape calculation, the more perfectly it develops" (Rheinstein, 1968, pp. 215–216). Worse yet, most modern organizational practices are designed and enacted as if these assumptions were correct.

For example, following from the inaccurate assumptions about people contained in the TFW virus, managers treated important functional processes, such as operations and sales, the same way they treated machines, cash, and other factors of production. Key work processes were judged in terms of their efficiency, reliability, and down time, a set of criteria consistent with a mechanistic view of organizations (Morgan, 1997). Latter day followers of Taylor, Fayol, and Weber, such as Shingo or

Hammer and Champy, furthered these traditional principles of organization design and the division of work with the principles of ongoing process improvement (Hammer & Champy, 1993; Shingo, 1988). They proposed innovative ideas and collaborated with others to create concepts of seamless functioning, such as Lean-6 Sigma and reengineering. That is, even though these researchers did not intend to dehumanize organizations, the unintended consequences of their assumptions about the nature of human capital resulted in unaddressed organizational dysfunctions, such as occupational stress and disease, turnover, and low productivity. The improper implementation of systems, structures, and processes was not the result of bad intentions; it resulted from the lack of intention and management will to recognize and challenge the inherent assumptions that dehumanized and over-engineered organizations.

An important implication of the socio-economic theory of organizations is that when organizations possess the TFW virus and pursue growth and efficiency under traditional principles, they develop a variety of dysfunctions that actually hide waste and inefficiency. Some of this waste and inefficiency is visible in the form of actual costs, and some of it is truly "hidden." On the visible side, the expected effectiveness and efficiency of automating work processes can result in measurable productivity losses or excess implementation costs if there is no associated training intervention with employees. In other cases, much of the waste from growth and the pursuit of efficiency are hidden in the sense that many of the costs are not captured (or perhaps buried) in income statements or statements of cash flow.

Consider the classic story of the little Dutch boy who discovers a hole in the dike and prevents the city from flooding by plugging the hole with his finger. In the morning, the townspeople come out, fix the dike, and relieve the Dutch boy of his burden. It is a story of sacrifice, empowerment, and effectiveness. In organizations with the TRW virus, however, instead of fixing the dike, the organization uses available investment capital to build more dikes and, as more holes in the original dike emerge, it finds more people to put their fingers in the holes, develops a system to support these heroic individuals, and comes to believe that this hole-plugging system is normal. It replicates the hole-plugging system when holes appear in other dikes. Hidden costs represent all the effort expended to plug the holes that no one sees as a problem because the dike appears to be working fine. In the pursuit of scale economies and the efficient use of physical capital, a whole system of non-value-added and unempowered work is created.

Hidden costs refer to the economic implications of organization dysfunctions—holes in the dike—that the misguided objectives of the TFW virus ignore. These dysfunctions are "handled" by decisions and actions—finding more people to plug holes—to correct the harmful/negative effects of the dysfunction on organization effectiveness and employee satisfaction, rather than fixing the hole itself.

According to Savall's approach (Savall, 2003), organizations identify hidden costs by exploring indicators of dysfunction, such as absenteeism, turnover, and productivity gaps. These indicators are symptoms, not root causes but signals, of a deeper problem. For instance, a fever may be the symptom of an infection, just as absenteeism may be the symptom of people occupying work that has little meaning or significance which, in turn, may be due to an unfixed hole in the dike. To handle the fever, the patient can take aspirin, but this will not eliminate the infection, and a few hours later the fever returns. To handle absenteeism among the "hole pluggers," the company can provide additional benefits or increase wages, but this will not prevent the absenteeism tomorrow or fix the dike. Thus, there is a big difference between "handling" a dysfunction, which involves a short-term, costly, and ultimately unnecessary action, and "converting" these unnecessary actions and dysfunctions into value-added activity. This would involve allowing the hole pluggers to fix the dike and then giving them more meaningful work. The socio-economic theory of organizations suggests that the hidden costs resulting from organization dysfunction—the excessive fragmentation of tasks, the over-specialization of functions, and the resulting additional organizational systems built up to address the dysfunction—can cancel out the expected gains from new strategic initiatives. Organization dysfunctions and hidden costs represent the depletion of human energy without the creation of value-add.

As a result, the socio-economic theory of organizations argues that systems infected with the TFW virus cannot develop the ability to spontaneously adapt to their environment. Instead, organizations are likely to develop a set of dysfunctions and operate at lower levels of performance. The ineffectiveness and inefficiency in decision making and information processing are generally not recognized, and management processes are put in place to monitor and regulate the dysfunction.

Combatting the TFW Virus

To bring a balance to the way organizations are designed and to provide a platform for practice, Savall created a socio-economic theory of organizations (Savall, 1974, 1980). It challenged many of the primary assumptions and implications of Taylor, Fayol, and Weber, and introduced an alternative set of assumptions regarding people and their potentially important contribution to organizational effectiveness. He also challenged some basic assumptions of economic theory.

For example, Savall and his colleagues suggested that there was an implicit assumption in economic theory that all forms of capital—labor, physical/technological, and financial—were equivalent in terms of their ability to produce economic value. While all forms of capital are important sources of value, physical and technical capital depreciate over time, and while financial capital can grow, it is not capable of directing itself. Savall argued that only human capital, and its ability and potential for creativity, can develop or destroy, leverage or waste, exploit or ignore other sources of value.

For this reason, human capital—the present value of the skills, knowledge, experience, and competencies of the workforce—is difficult to calculate because of its potential to be more than just the discounted flow of future skill and competency value. That is the assumption of the TFW virus and standard economic theory. When textbooks list labor among other forms of capital, the unstated assumption is that labor is equivalent to commodities, and the implication is that only a few organizational members can be clever, strategic thinkers. The socio-economic theory of organizations assumes that all employees, regardless of level in the hierarchy, are capable of innovation. As a result, the socio-economic theory of organizations prefers to pursue the optimization of *human potential.*

Organizations tap into the potential of human capital through the development and negotiation of appropriate and aspirational purposes and objectives. Indeed, the lack of agreement on purpose and objectives among organizational members, in particular those members in the vertical hierarchy, can result in a number of operational and strategic dysfunctions, including poor decision making, inefficient product and service development processes, and disengaged talent. Developing human potential involves arranging structures, systems, and processes in service of these purposes and objectives. Thus, human potential is partly a function of its capacity to cooperate and the quality of the teamwork among its members to create value through challenging objectives.

However, traditional management tools and managerial skills rooted in the TFW virus are more focused on leveraging passive factors of value creation—physical, financial, and intellectual capital—under inappropriate assumptions about the nature of human capital and potential. As a result, traditional management tools must be updated to become more comprehensive, and the socio-economic theory of organizations proposes that tools and processes can be developed and implemented to enhance and leverage the value of an organization's human potential. The productive and enlightened management of people became the heart of the socio-economic theory of organizations.

To preserve or even develop its capacity for short-, medium-, and long-term survival, development, and competitiveness, the organization must intentionally implement a new kind of management system. The experiments carried out by ISEOR's research teams in over 1,310 companies and organizations demonstrate that poor relationships among organization members result in inefficient change processes as well as resistance to processes aimed at converting hidden costs into value-added activities. Organizing in ways that tap human potential speeds up the process of converting dysfunctions resulting from the TFW virus into value-added work, of transforming low-added-value activities into high-added-value activity, and of liberating socio-economic performance.

Overview of the Book

Demonstrating how organization agility can be achieved through the application of the socio-economic theory of organizations is the primary purpose of this book. Organizations can choose to operate in a manner similar to JCDecaux or in a way that reflects dysfunctions and hidden costs that harm people and destroy value added.

Most examples of agility focus on large, public companies. The stories of Google, Zara, and Unilever are well documented in business school cases. On the other hand, there are embarrassingly few examples of the agility implementation and they are also about large, public firms. The transformations of ABB, IBM, and Nokia are the subject of book-length cases and bloggers everywhere. In addition, there tends to be a U.S. bias in most professional business books, where the stories of Southwest Airlines, Starbucks, UPS, and Apple are told. There is a dearth of examples of how agility develops in general, how smaller, closely held firms evolve the agile capability, and how non-U.S. organizations implement agility. There is an important need to demonstrate the concept of agility and the transformation to agility in a very different culture and economy.

We think the Brioche Pasquier Group (BPG) case is a great example to fill that gap. In Chapter 2, we describe BPG and show how the socio-economic approach to management (SEAM) was used to build flexible management practices that supported the organization's growth and its development of the agile capability. Chapter 3 continues the Brioche Pasquier case and the company's experience in applying the SEAM methodology to its internationalization. This longitudinal view provides an opportunity to see the SEAM process in action and how it builds the agile routines and capability. In particular, BPG's expansion across Europe and then into the U.S. market provides the opportunity to demonstrate how learning and change implementation were applied.

Chapter 4 reflects on and discusses the BPG case. It provides important learnings and recommendations for organizations that want to become agile organizations.

References

Buono, A., & Savall, H. (2015). *The socio-economic approach to management revisited: The evolving nature of SEAM in the 21st century.* Charlotte, NC: Information Age.

Christensen, C. (1997). *The innovator's dilemma: When new technologies cause great firms to fail.* Boston, MA: Harvard Business School Press.

D'Aveni, R. (1994). *Hypercompetition.* New York: The Free Press.

D'Aveni, R., Dagnino, G., and Smith, K. (2010). "The age of temporary advantage." *Strategic Management Journal, 31*(3), 1371–1385.

Haeckel, S. (1999). *Adaptive enterprise: Creating and leading sense-and-respond organizations.* Boston. MA: Harvard Business School Press.

Hammer, M., and Champy, J. (1993). *Reengineering the corporation.* New York: HarperCollins.

i4cp.com. (2014). www.i4cp.com/trendwatchers/2014/04/16/ from-march-madness-to-market-madness-building-agile-workforce-planning-and-analytics-capability

Katz, D., and Kahn, R. L. (1978). *The social psychology of organizations* (2nd ed.). Hoboken, NJ: John Wiley & Sons.

Lant, T., and Mezias, S. (1992). "An organizational learning model of convergence and reorientation." *Organization Science*, 3, pp. 47–71.

McGahan, A. M. (1999). "Competition, strategy, and business performance." *California Management Review*, 41(3), 74–101.

McGahan, A. M. (1999). "The performance of US corporations: 1981–1994." *Journal of Industrial Economics*, 47(4), 373–398.

McGregor, D. (1960). *The human side of enterprise*. New York: McGraw-Hill.

Morgan, G. (1997). *Images of organization*. Thousand Oaks, CA: Sage.

Perrow, C. (1971). *Complex organizations: A critical essay*. Chicago, IL: Scott Foresman.

Rheinstein, M. (Ed.). (1968). *Max Weber on law in economy and society* (E.Shils & M.Rheinstein, Trans.). New York: Simon and Schuster, p. 223.

Rheinstein, M. (Ed.). (1968). *Max Weber on law in economy and society* (E.Shils & M.Rheinstein, Trans.). New York: Simon and Schuster, pp. 215–216).

Richard, P. Devinney, T., Yip, G., and Johnson, G. (2009). "Measuring organizational performance: Toward methodological best practice." *Journal of Management*, 35(3), 718–804.

Romanelli, E., and Tushman, M. (1994). "Organizational transformation as punctuated equilibrium: An empirical test." *Academy of Management Journal*, 37, 1141–1166.

Savall, H. (1974, 1981). *Work and people: An economic evaluation of job-enrichment* (2nd ed.). Charlotte, NC: Information Age.

(Original work published in French in 1974, and in English in 1981).

Savall, H. (2003). "An updated presentation of the socio-economic management model and its international dissemination." *Journal of Organizational Change Management, 16*(1), 33–48.

Savall, H., & Zardet, V. (2008). *Mastering hidden costs and socioeconomic performance*. Charlotte, NC: Information Age Publishing. (First published in French in 1987.)

Savall, H., & Zardet, V. (2012). New statement of the socioeconomic theory of organizations and territories. Working paper, ISEOR, Lyon, France.

Shingo, S. (1988). *Non-stock production: The Shingo system of continuous improvement*. New York: Productivity Press.

Steers, S. (1975). "Problems in the measurement of organization effectiveness." *Administrative Science Quarterly, 10*, pp. 546–558.

Sull, D. (2008). *The upside of turbulence*. New York: Harper Business Press.

Trist, E., and Bamforth, K. (1951). "Some social and psychological consequences of the longwall method of coal-getting." *Human Relations, 4*, pp. 3–38.

Tushman, M., and Anderson, P. (1986). "Technological discontinuities and organizational environments." *Administrative Science Quarterly*, pp. 439–465.

Tushman, M., and O'Reilly, C. (1996). "Ambidextrous organizations: Managing evolutionary and revolutionary change." *California Management Review, 38*, pp. 8–30.

Volberda, H. (1998). *Building the flexible firm: How to remain competitive*. New York: Oxford University Press.

Whittington, R., Pettigrew, A., Peck, S. Fenton, E., and Conyon, M. (1999). "Change and complementarities in the new competitive landscape: A European panel study, 1992–1996." *Organization Science*, *10*(5), 583–600.

Worley, C., and Mohrman, S. (2014). "Is change management obsolete?" *Organizational Dynamics*, *43*(3), 214–224.

Worley, C., Williams, T., and Lawler, E.E., III. (2014). *The agility factor*. San Francisco, CA: Jossey-Bass.

2

The Beginnings of Agility at Brioche Pasquier

The people of France—to no one's surprise—have a love affair with food, and one of the essential elements is bread. From the denser, everyday baguette to the more delicate brioches and pastries served for breakfast or dessert, breads of all sorts are a staple of French life.

The Brioche Pasquier Group was formed in a very simple way by Serge and Louis-Marie Pasquier in 1974. It initially produced both bread and brioche. A year later, due to the success of the business, they stopped making bread to focus exclusively on brioche. Louis-Marie, the eldest, traveled extensively to distribute the products; Serge was in charge of accounting. They quickly realized that the ubiquitous village bakery was too small and the industry too fragmented to be able to meet the growing demand. Philippe and François-Xavier Pasquier joined the organization in charge of manufacturing the products. Pascal, the youngest, joined his brothers in 1977 to take sales responsibilities.

From the beginning, the company's product/market strategy prioritized quality and freshness. All of BPG's products were sold fresh and usually consumed within a couple of days (although the product could last up to three weeks). BPG worked closely with local customers, sourced ingredients locally, and used no artificial colors or flavoring. Because sources and customers were local, the organization prided itself on its small ecological footprint.

The company distributed brioches through a commercial channel consisting of small independent stores and large supermarket chains (although they eventually dropped the small store channel to focus only on mass distribution). The core, mass distribution channel, however, was highly competitive. Many, if not all, of these retailers had aggressive supplier policies that pressured vendors for the lowest prices, a practice that continues today.

As a family business, BPG promoted and practiced humanistic values and focused on long-term as well as short-term performance. Unlike many traditional French firms—where the TFW virus is alive and well—BPG's leaders were concerned about people and profitability. By 1984, the family business's 240 employees produced, marketed, sold, and distributed brioche products from a single, functionally organized site near the western city of Cholet, France (Figure 2.1). Profitability during its first ten years was high, compounded growth rates were above 20 percent, and regional market shares and BPG's brand in western France were growing. Its balanced view of the business and its concerted efforts to listen to customers is part of what made BPG such a unique element of the French economy.

Nineteen eighty-four was also when senior management at BPG believed the time was right to think carefully about the organization, its growth, and the eventual handing over of company control to the next generation of Pasquiers. The

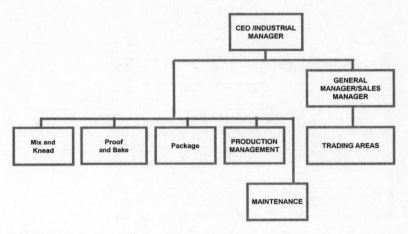

Figure 2.1   BPG Organization Chart (1984)

main issues were not only how to continue growing but how to manage the risk associated with losing control of this growth. In keeping with the family culture, BPG wanted to prevent the organization from turning into a bloated, headquarters-heavy, centralized bureaucracy where managers and employees were stifled, uncreative, and unfulfilled.

The family was keen on ensuring the sustainability of the business and its financial independence, although it did join a regional stock exchange in 1985. For twenty-one years, it offered 20 percent of its equity to the public to access needed investment capital to fund growth plans. For example, the firm used investment capital to build a new site in eastern France in 1988 (Figure 2.2). Management organized and operated the plant using the same principles that preserved the quality, freshness, and ecological strategies but also adopted lessons learned from the initial socio-economic interventions described below.

Finally, BPG wanted to prepare for the CEO's succession, who was, at that time, still young (twenty-eight). The desire of the family to enable a peaceful CEO transition required a

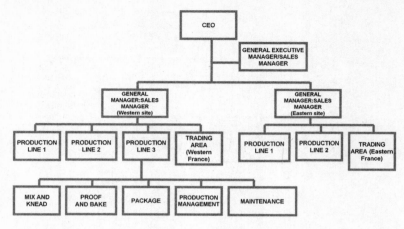

Figure 2.2   BPG Organizational Chart (1988)

thoughtful discussion about how best to make investment decisions to support the expectations of any successor.

BPG and the SEAM Methodology

Drawing on the socio-economic theory of organizations described in Chapter 1, the socio-economic approach to management (SEAM) methodology is a form of action research (Savall & Zardet, 2014). Simply put, action research is a cyclical approach to organization development and change management that takes action based on evidence and learning. SEAM has a long history of success that owes to its structured approach to action research. The typical bureaucratic culture finds the implementation logic clear; SEAM's attention to detail eliminates much of the uncertainty associated with large-scale change. While based on applied intervention-research, the implementation process is practical, operational, and useful to managers and executives.

BPG's organization values coincided with the key values of action research and the SEAM approach: empowerment, high involvement on development objectives, trusting employees to enhance intrapreneurship, and appreciation of the individual's contribution to collective company performance (Pasquier & Pasquier, 2012). BPG leaders chose the SEAM approach because of its consistency and compatibility with their views regarding the enhancement of economic and social performance.

"When the ISEOR researchers began to work with us, we thought the company was like a boat. The advantage or the drawback of this boat metaphor was that, once out at sea, we could not allow ourselves to leave it. We were all together. It is not always simple and easy, but it allowed us, in hard times as well as in prosperous ones, to keep unity and solidarity." (Serge Pasquier, 2011)

As shown in Figure 2.3, the metaphorical objective of the change was to get from one shore to another. But how that objective would be achieved—the strategy—could take a variety of forms or paths. BPG's use of the SEAM methodology represented one of those paths.

The SEAM methodology proposes that effective organizations apply and integrate three categories of change activity (Table 2.1). The *improvement process* describes the overall and

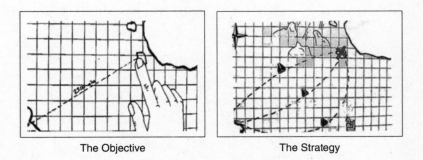

      The Objective   The Strategy

Figure 2.3 BPG's Goal and Strategy

Source: Strategy and objective charts. © 2013, Brioche Pasquier. Used with permission.

Table 2.1 The SEAM Framework*

SEAM Category	Definition	Specific Elements or Processes
Improvement Process	A closed-loop change cycle aimed at learning from dysfunctions to convert hidden costs into value-added activities and instill an ethic of constant change	• Diagnosis • Project and focus group action planning • Implementation • Evaluation
Socio-Economic Management Tools	A set of templates and processes aimed at expanding the scope of typical management tools by integrating human potential and establishing a coherent management system	• Internal-External Strategic Action Plan • Priority Action Plan • Time Management • Competency Grid • Strategic Piloting Logbook • Periodically Negotiable Activity Contract

| Strategic and Political Decisions | The choices an organization makes, in line with its values, and in specific settings. The choices should be clear, formal, and transparent. They represent the targets of intervention activity. | • Breadth of product line, markets served, technologies used, or regions of operation
• Levels of risk, speed, and investment aggressiveness
• Organization structures
• Human potential development policy
• Organizational purpose and values
• Decision rights
• Planning, budgeting, and resource allocation processes |

* Adapted from H. Savall & V. Zardet. *Mastering hidden costs and socio-economic performance*. Charlotte, NC: Information Age, 2008.

recurring activities of change and learning. It is a straightforward and participative cycle of diagnosis, the development of projects, implementation, and evaluation activities. Within the improvement process, a variety of *socio-economic management tools*, such as priority action plans and periodically negotiable activity contracts, help to align the *strategic and political dimensions* of the organization. That is, strategic and political decisions, such as product breadth, the type of structures used, and incentive systems employed, describe the targets of intervention, but it is the improvement process and the management tools that really define the activities of a SEAM process.

The Initial Improvement Process at BPG

The improvement process guides SEAM interventions. Similar to the Shewhart cycle of "plan-do-check-act," the improvement process instills in the organization a belief that change is constant and normal. However, it differs from total quality management or other continuous improvement approaches in that it operates at the organization- or business-unit level rather than on specific processes. Optimizing individual processes can often result in a variety of dysfunctions and sub-optimization at the organization level. Approaching change at the organization level triggers a shift in the way people think about their environment.

The Diagnostic Process

The initial SEAM intervention program at BPG began in 1984 with ISEOR researchers interviewing nearly all of the employees and managers at its original Les Cerqueux (near Cholet) site. They developed a comprehensive inventory of the dysfunctions harming value-add and human resource activities. Quotes from the interviews were categorized according to six dysfunction categories that ISEOR researchers have found repeatedly: working conditions, work organization, communication-coordination-cooperation, time management, integrated training, and strategy implementation (Table 2.2).

SEAM's diagnostic focus on the identification of dysfunctions and "hidden costs" is unique. The rules, policies, and systems that make up these dysfunctions and reinforce their continued presence are costly for the organization. They are "hidden" in the sense that they are not captured by accounting or other management systems, and yet they hurt organizational productivity and efficiency.

Hidden costs are like the extra heat generated by an inefficient engine. All engines produce heat that results from different parts rubbing together and creating friction. There are inherent inefficiencies and waste in even the most finely tuned and well-designed engines. But inefficient engines produce even more heat and, as a result, waste fuel and wear out parts faster. If you know where to look and how to measure the higher than expected heat, direct action can be taken to reduce the rubbing among the parts and avoid energy waste. Rather than seeing frequent part failures and the resulting replacement costs as normal, the alignment of the parts can be improved, engine performance increased, and parts expense decreased.

Hidden costs are symptoms of long-run inefficiency and managerial short-sightedness. ISEOR researchers have

Table 2.2 Dysfunction Categories in the SEAM Methodology

Dysfunction Category	Definition	Possible Sample Comments
Working Conditions	The physical working environment	The factory is noisy and lacks air conditioning
Work Organization	The way work is designed and performed	Procedures are not clear or contradict each other
Communication-Coordination-Cooperation	How management and employees integrate work processes, direction setting, and decision making	Customer claims are not being properly reported by sales reps to the marketing managers, resulting in complaints, order errors, and late deliveries
Time Management	How supervisors, managers, and executives spend their time	Disruptions during important meetings due to phone calls and people checking e-mails
Integrated Training	Programs, to improve organization members skills, knowledge, and competencies	Investments in new equipment are made without enough explanation or training regarding its proper handling nor the safety rules
Strategy Implementation	The way strategic objectives are translated into action, including the tools and decisions that support them (e.g., IT and investments)	Objectives are not clearly explained, and there is misunderstanding regarding the urgent need to develop new products

demonstrated that most companies are absorbing a small fortune in "hidden costs." The overall amount of hidden costs can range from 25 to 50 percent of the company's value added, and often more than the payroll. These costs do not show up as distinct expenses, and yet traditional management systems reinforce the behavior associated with them. For example, when an *additional* 10 percent of the skilled workforce left an organization following the implementation of a business process reengineering project aimed at reducing staff, managers believed that they had exceeded the goals of the project because salary costs were lower than projected. However, the organization was operating below optimum staffing levels. These lower staffing levels increased stress among the remaining employees, who attempted to meet unchanged production quotas, but did so at a great social and, eventually, financial cost. Deliberately converting hidden costs into value-added activity—in this case, hiring enough skilled workers to staff the process appropriately—represents a commitment to organizational learning and company health.

The main symptoms of hidden costs stemming from dysfunctions include absenteeism, work accidents and occupational illness, staff turnover, "non-quality" (e.g., quality defects, delivery delays, returns, customer complaints, and so forth), and productivity gaps (Table 2.3).

As in all SEAM interventions, hidden costs were calculated at BPG by working from the dysfunctions gathered in the interviews and mapping them out in a chart of qualitative, quantitative, and financial impacts. The calculation method associated with hidden costs is based on a

Table 2.3 Hidden Cost Indicators

Symptoms of Hidden Costs	Example
Absenteeism	An employee calls in sick rather than coming into an office that is overheated
Work accidents and occupational illness	Employee medical costs resulting from on-the-job injuries from the new equipment
Turnover	After a takeover, some of the most skilled and highly performing employees resign and are hired by a competitor
Quality defects	A customer switches to a competitor because of better service (the lack of a response to the complaint)
Productivity gaps	Idle time due to bug-laden software Wasted effort because objectives were not clear and the line of sight between work effort and strategy was not established

socio-economic principle developed by the ISEOR researchers called "qualimetrics" or taking qualitative information and translating it into financial figures (Savall & Zardet, 2011). It is different from other approaches to estimating cost savings because hidden costs are not only extra costs, but also earnings losses and opportunity costs. Organization members and the ISEOR consultants pinpoint the costs or earnings losses and agree on the financial amounts that result from the various actions implemented to handle the dysfunctions. Table 2.4 summarizes several of the hidden costs identified in the 1984 diagnosis.

Table 2.4 Example of Hidden Costs Per Person Per Year in the 1984 Diagnosis (in 2014 USD)

Symptoms	Qualitative Assessment	Quantitative Assessment	Financial Assessment
Absenteeism and work accidents	High rates in packaging department Little safety training	5.8% of absenteeism	$5,400
Staff turnover	Not assessed	Not assessed	Not assessed
"Non-quality" (e.g., quality problems)	Scrapped dough	21 tons/year	$3,700
	Unsold or recalled products	1% of the products	$1,300
	Loss of raw material	75 tons/year	$1,400
	Production losses	4% of the annual production	$5,200
Direct productivity gap	Frequent excess weight	50 tons/year	$2,600
	Machine failures	20h/month	$13,000
Total hidden costs per person per year			$32,600

Source: © ISEOR 1985. Used with permission.

Every symptom of hidden costs identified in the interviews is estimated, and the numbers can be staggering. For example, as shown in the circled portion of Table 2.4, the interviews addressed several kinds of production losses.

Production Waste Calculation

• Crushed products at the end of the production line	2,000 pieces/day
• Fallen products at the end of the oven	200 per day
• Damaged products due to the gap between the backing trays	1,000 per day
• Burnt, badly formed, badly cooked, badly gilded products	500 per day
• Crushed products during transportation	200 per day
• Crumpled packaging	100 per day
Amount of products that could have been sold	4,000 pieces/day

Production Loss Calculation

• Manufacturing failures	1,000 per month
• Daily manufacturing delays	200 per month (e.g., personnel scheduling, low coordination between departments, informal management styles)
Amount of products not produced	1,200 pieces/month

In consultation with managers and production experts, ISEOR evaluated two kinds of production losses:

Product waste: 4,000 pieces a day × 313 days a year = 1,252,000 pieces
Production loss: 1,200 a month × 12 months = 14,400 pieces

BPG calculated the value of the product waste by using the sales revenue (e.g., $0.42/piece) the company was losing by throwing away these products. The value of production loss was calculated using only the margin lost, since the company did not consume the raw material and the production time (e.g., $0.42 × 40%).

Hidden costs related to product waste: $1,252,000 × \$0.42 = \$525,840$
Hidden costs related to production loss: $14,400 × 0.42\$ × 40\% = \$2,419$
Total amount of production losses $= \$528,300$
Total amount per person per year (assuming 100 people in the factory) $= \$5,200$

This last amount appears in Table 2.4, at the line "production losses" and represents around 4 percent of the annual production volume.

In each company, dozens and often hundreds of calculation sheets like the example above are developed and summed. Such a calculation process stands in contrast to traditional approaches that are more one-sided and top-down, and brings evidence to decision-makers that a singular focus on cutting visible costs may be misleading or wrong. As a result, approaching hidden costs in this manner results in internal commitment to converting those costs and unnecessary behaviors into value-added activity. Top-down approaches usually result in resistance to change and value destruction when intended actions are implemented poorly or sabotaged and contribute to the cycle of dysfunction. This is the primary reason why business process reengineering and lean/six sigma approaches that claim millions and millions of dollars of cost savings are never able to point to these savings in cash flow statements, income statements, or balance sheets.

Action Planning and Implementation

The second and third steps in SEAM's improvement process continued at BPG in 1986 with the development and implementation of specific projects. It began with focus groups designing innovative solutions, driving the transformation of hidden costs into value-added activities, and improving performance.

The SEAM method focuses simultaneously on designing and implementing both horizontal and vertical change processes. Horizontal changes support the transformation of hidden costs into value-added work through social and managerial performance improvements. Horizontal interventions involve management teams and cross-functional (that is, lateral, horizontal, or transverse) processes. Involving senior managers in the identification and design of coordination processes across functions, business units, geographies, or other core structural features is critical. Vertical changes involve work within a function or business unit and typically address strategic objectives of economic value. Such an intervention architecture derives from a belief that embedding change within an organization, from the C-suite to the shop floor, requires both types of work.

This horizontal-vertical approach, what the ISEOR scientists call the HORIVERT principle (Figure 2.4), is an overarching standard that governs and integrates a company's managerial processes. It helps to align the projects designed at top management team levels with those proposed by focus groups in various departments of the company. This promotes collective learning and team integration, two important sources of effective and efficient operations.

HORIZONTAL ACTION: Collaborative training of the management and supervisory team with a view to using socio-economic management tools focused on work that crosses functions, products or regions

VERTICAL ACTION: Diagnoses and projects within a functional, product, or regional sector

Figure 2.4   The HORIVERT Model

Source: © ISEOR, 1985. Used with permission.

BPG's Initial Horizontal Intervention

The initial horizontal intervention to address the hidden costs focused on changing the way BPG managed the site organization. The SEAM approach is not a narrow-minded attempt to eliminate waste; the approach is not about driving out hidden costs in the pursuit of efficiency. Rather, the focus of the approach is on understanding the sources of hidden costs and converting those processes and decisions into value-added activities. That might mean making a process more efficient, but it can also mean using the slack resources implied by hidden costs to develop future opportunities.

All BPG managers and supervisors were involved in a training program that introduced the socio-economic management tools, including the time management tool, the internal/external strategic action plan, priority action plans, competency grids, and periodically negotiable activity contracts (Buono & Savall, 2007; Savall & Zardet, 2008; Savall, Zardet, & Bonnet, 2012). New managers hired by the company were trained by existing managers. The socio-economic management tools then were assembled into a six-month planning and operations cycle—a key element in the strategic and political decisions category (Table 2.1).

Strategic and political decisions comprise the direction setting, operational, structural, and human resource design features of the organization. They also include the alignment among the company's owners and members' values and the strategy's intentions regarding products, markets, technologies, and human potential. Decisions regarding the coherence among strategy, structure, systems, and processes required to support the involvement of all organization members in strategy implementation are a central intervention target in the SEAM approach. Even traditional organization design principles suggest that organizational choices regarding work design and job enrichment, coordination, innovation, reward systems, and leadership development should be aligned with each other and with the strategy (Galbraith, 2002).

The new planning system was built around a rolling three-year internal/external strategic action plan developed at the enterprise level and updated annually. The SEAM method assumes that employees are central to the current and future performance of the company, and they give (or withhold) their say and energy in service of that pursuit. As a result, the internal-external strategic action plan is created with high levels of involvement. Most established organizations have a planning process that results in a budget or set of initiatives for the next year. These strategic plans tend to be driven from the top and focused on production/service capabilities and financial objectives. Such a process and focus engenders resistance to change and creates hidden costs because top executives have not involved the people who will execute the plan. SEAM's internal-external strategic action plan augments this process by clarifying the scope of strategy implementation activities and outcomes over a three-to-five-year period for multiple stakeholders.

At BPG, this high-level strategic action plan was then broken down into semi-annual priority actions plans (PAPs) for the site. The PAP tool creates the appropriate set of initiatives that will generate current and future socio-economic outcomes. It includes an inventory of the strategy deployment and improvement initiatives related to the reduction and prevention of dysfunctional practices. These different initiatives are prioritized; focus on actions concerning people's work, their team, or their department; and typically address solutions in the six dysfunction categories of working conditions, work organization, time management, communication-coordination-cooperation, integrated training, and strategy implementation.

PAP development begins with a two- or three-hour "dysfunctions mini-diagnosis," a bottoms-up process facilitated by each manager with his or her team every six months (Figure 2.5). The mini-diagnosis encourages employees to express the difficulties, defects, and dysfunctions encountered in their work. In organizations where the TFW virus is strong

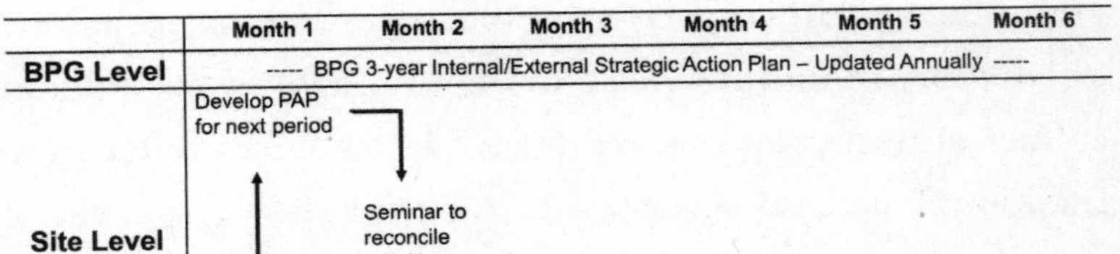

	Month 1	Month 2	Month 3	Month 4	Month 5	Month 6
BPG Level	----- BPG 3-year Internal/External Strategic Action Plan – Updated Annually -----					
Site Level	Develop PAP for next period	Seminar to reconcile priorities Coordination Seminar				
Team Level	Mini-diagnosis of dysfunctions	Develop PNACs	Monthly team meeting to review progress			Assess PNACs

Figure 2.5   Semi-Annual Priority Planning Process

or where there is a great deal of mistrust between employees and management, these meetings are often initially unproductive. Management must be patient and consistent in seeking this information. This patience, in combination with actions taken in response to feedback, builds the trust necessary to generate important information and insight.

The output from these meetings was local improvement, dysfunction reduction, or dysfunction prevention interventions. The team managers propose these interventions to their supervisors for inclusion in the priority action plan. Following these meetings, the managers and supervisors convene to arbitrate and reconcile any contradictions or overloaded action plans, to synchronize cross-departmental actions, and to communicate priorities to the other departments. The meeting helps to improve awareness and coordination, strengthen service operations, and develop and support professional skills and behavior. In addition, the site runs a coordination seminar with the production managers and the key functional staff, validates the site's priority action plans, and starts a coordination process on the objectives and priority actions.

Even when organizations have a strategic plan and objectives in addition to their vision and mission, their strategic initiatives are often uncoordinated. Grass-roots efforts can appear without reference to other initiatives, resulting in confusion over priorities and wasted effort. PAPs differ from traditional management practices in their design as a set of participative, integrated projects that take into account the dysfunctions and hidden costs identified in the diagnosis. Indeed, traditional management control practices often attempt to limit visible cost increases by rejecting investment proposals from employees. On the other hand, the socio-economic management tools and processes enable employees to argue for the relevance of investing more in innovation.

The aligned PAPs are then broken down into the managers' semi-annual calendars. Each employee and his or her superior, including the management staff, develop a periodically negotiable activity contract (PNAC) to clarify objectives and the appropriate means to achieve them. Over the next six months, monthly team meetings are organized to report on team productivity and quality improvements (or losses), clarify future contract objectives, and future coordination efforts necessary to support priority actions.

Periodically negotiable activity contracts (PNAC) are one of the most important management tools in the SEAM methodology. As an individual-level tool, they formalize objectives and strategies to improve the work systems and processes inside and outside of the usual day-to-day tasks. The PNAC recognizes that some hidden costs are "slack resources" that can support the trying out of new ideas or problem solving. For example, hidden costs can "constitute potential reserves or budgetary maneuver margins for improving the enterprise's economic performance" (Savall & Zardet, 1987). PNACs can focus on improving current effectiveness or on the development of future potential.

At the end of a six-month cycle, these negotiable activity contracts are assessed. When the projects in the PNAC are aimed at converting hidden costs that constrain performance into value-added activities, a monetary bonus for achieving individual or team/collective objectives is distributed, funded by the amount of cost and value converted. As a result, this tool has replaced job descriptions in the company because it includes objectives related to both the short-term performance of the company and the creation of potential (development actions). The PNAC completes a coherent management system because the tools used (Internal/External Strategic Action Plan, Priority Action Plans, and PNACs) are prepared and validated through a negotiation process between top management, middle management, and employees and workers.

Figure 2.6 shows how the objective "increase autonomy of the sales development manager" in the internal/external strategic action plan was broken down by the sales manager and his or her team. Their proposal was to implement three main priority actions: (A) identify the salespeople for pilot training, (B) set up a new and autonomous sales team, and (C)

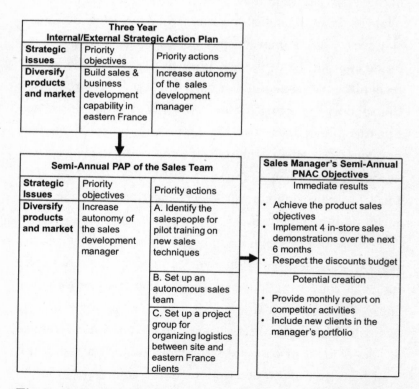

Figure 2.6 How BPG Links Key Management Tools

set up a logistics project. Then, when the sales manager negotiated the semi-annual PNACs with his or her salespeople, they concretely defined five objectives, three of which (Objectives 1, 2, and 3) were short-term oriented and two of which were intended to create future potential. The potential objectives are less traditional; they lead to actions that contribute to PAP objectives and prepare the organization for performance in the next few years. In this case, the "Provide monthly report" objective refers to a current developmental opportunity for this sales manager. The PNAC process provides the supervisor with the opportunity to explain the behavior (for example, lack of feedback) and to negotiate the objective to reinforce the importance of feedback.

In addition to the above process, BPG implemented three other SEAM tools—time management tools, competency grids, and piloting logbooks—during the first phase of the intervention. Together, they helped managers understand how to create time for development activities, served as a platform to develop training plans to increase the versatility of different teams, and provided an inventory of measures and metrics (and their values). They played an important role in synchronizing the PAPs and enhanced managers' ability to react to unexpected events. For example, the production department losses identified in the hidden costs evaluation became an indicator updated every day in the piloting logbooks, displayed easily by the supervisors, and served as a basis for developing needed skills.

Once this system was established at the original site, it was diffused to the other plant location. Eventually, as the organization grew in terms of sites and products, an additional layer of coordination was added so that the different site PAPs were synchronized and the organization was optimizing its resources and activities.

BPG's Initial Vertical Intervention

After the initial diagnosis of dysfunctions and hidden costs (see Table 2.4), ISEOR consultants, managers, and employees were aware of the need to reorganize BPG's production processes. From the beginning, BPG's brioche production process had been organized functionally. Separate departments for mixing and kneading the dough, baking the bread, packaging products, and maintaining the equipment reported to functional managers. A production line consisted of sequential tasks from the three departments to meet a specific order (see Figure 2.7, "Before").

A cross-functional group brought together to think through the problems believed that efficiencies might be gained by self-containing the process and pivoting managerial control to a production line manager. Figure 2.7, "After," shows how the focus group thought about the change. By creating self-contained production lines, each line "owned" its own kneading, baking, and packaging processes, as well as the equipment maintenance functions necessary to keep the lines running smoothly. Each production line was to have annual, semiannual, and monthly objectives for productivity and quality that would complement the emerging planning process described earlier. In addition, each line would be responsible for the creation of objectives related to future potential. Although this approach is common today under the banner of self-managed teams, it was a radical idea in 1984.

Guiding people to engage in new behaviors is a key success factor during the implementation phase. For example, imple-

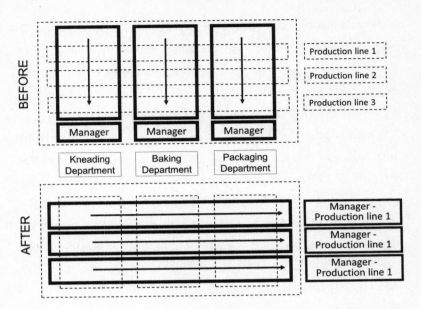

Figure 2.7 Redesigning the Brioche Production Process (Before and After)

menting the new production system involved monthly meetings to coach managers through the transition. Report-outs to top management were made to track progress or when help was needed to remove roadblocks. In this case, bakers were often reluctant to own the maintenance of their equipment. They argued that they had not been hired to adjust or maintain ovens. However, a variety of hidden costs (see Table 2.4) were related to a lack of safety training on certain machines, frequent changes in production personnel working hours, a high degree of compartmentalization between baking and packaging, little integrated training, and unqualified workers. As a result, the CEO made it clear—and emphasized—that a flexible, multiskilled, and safe workforce was key to the new strategy at BPG.

A second vertical intervention was conducted in 1988 at the second site in eastern France. The plant had manifest a variety of problems within two months of coming online. A partial set of diagnostic hidden costs is shown in Table 2.5. As the production process changes described above were being implemented in the second plant, an additional set of actions, including shutting down a production line, were taken.

A third vertical intervention with the sales teams from both plants was delivered in 1988. The estimated hidden costs of $13,800 per person per year were due to absenteeism, personnel turnover, non-quality, and direct productivity gaps, including product loss, late deliveries, and unresolved disputes. Direct productivity gaps accounted for 80 percent of the hidden costs. The main improvement actions conceived by the project group are presented in Table 2.6.

Evaluating the Initial Intervention

Evaluation is the fourth step in the improvement process. An assessment of the plant's conversion of hidden costs into value-added activity showed improvements of $19,000 per

Table 2.5 Hidden Costs in the Second Site (Partial Assessment Per Person Per Year)

Hidden Costs	Amount
Non-quality	
*Breakdowns	$ 3,200
*Crushed products during transportation, crumpled packaging	$ 1,900
Direct productivity gaps	
*Overproduction on one line	$ 6,300
*Underproduction on another line	$ 4,300
Total hidden costs per person per year	$15,700

Source: © ISEOR 1987

Table 2.6 Improvement Actions in the Sales Teams

Dysfunction Category	Actions
Work conditions	Investment in a new ordering and stock management software program for reducing ordering errors
Work organization	Redistribute and delegate tasks between sales manager and salespeople
Communication-coordination-cooperation	Monthly meetings between sales managers, salespeople, and sales promoters to coordinate store demonstration and share information about competitor actions and behaviors (i.e., prices, promotion, events) A rotation program for salesmen between the plants and the head office
Integrated training	Implementation of welcoming and integration programs for the new salesmen to reduce turnover Appointment of a mentor/sponsor for each new salesman during their initial few months of employment.

person per year (Table 2.7). The original site's reorganization of the production function increased flexibility, stabilized production schedules and working hours, and enhanced trust in managerial roles. Improvements in safety and health and the shutdown of a losing production line also contributed.

In addition, BPG integrated the use of hidden costs and risks into its decision making. That is, while calculating hidden costs is useful, the concept can be applied generically in overall problem solving as well. For example, with respect to logistics and distribution issues, BPG recognized that a key point of control was not whether trucks left the factory full of goods

Table 2.7 Evaluation of Hidden Cost Conversion for Production Processes (1987, Per Person Per Year)

Symptom	Qualitative Outcomes	Quantitative Outcomes	Financial Contribution
Absenteeism and work accidents	Greater motivation Better working hours Better training and awareness of risks of accidents	Absenteeism at packaging down 1%	$1,200
Nonquality	Best handling of faults and defects Fewer scrapped articles	Losses down 0.5% Improvement in quality: recall rate down 0.5%	$1,300 $2,500
Direct productivity gap	Socio-economic organization model introduced based on product lines	2% of gains per day Removal of a loss-making line related to improved management tools Timesaving in the organization of production Less maintenance work	$3,000 $5,000 $4,000 $2,000
Total conversion of hidden costs per person per year			$19,000

Source: © ISEOR, 1987

but that an order was delivered on time. A focus on the visible costs of truckload utilization clouded decisions related to freshness and on-time delivery. In fact, it was delivery consistency and punctuality, not a fully loaded truck, which resulted in sustainable economic performance.

At the end of the first year, Brioche Pasquier showed important improvements in economic performance (Savall & Zardet, 2008). Absenteeism dropped from 4.5 percent to 1.5 percent, staff turnover declined from 90 percent to 11 percent, and quality improved, resulting in a 7.9 percent profitability increase. This increase in profitability occurred despite the time, efforts, and costs associated with implementing the improvement projects and supported the conclusion that the performance improvements had clearly exceeded the amount of investment.

Company executives explained their success in terms of two main factors.

"The company's historical key success factor is first of all its product. We inherited it from our parents; it is of an excellent quality and is greatly appreciated by customers and consumers. The second factor consists of two fundamental choices: the choice to stay close to the customer thanks to our decentralized organizational system, and the choice to work directly with mass distributors. We are aware that our brioche is good as long as it is fresh. It explains the relevance of shortening all the circuits: logistics, supply chain, for getting closer to the consumers." (Pascal Pasquier, 2012)

The decentralized organization system enabled the company to connect with its customers. The ISEOR approach—both the horizontal changes to planning, including the PNACs, and the vertical changes to production—allowed the organization to work closely and directly with the large retailers. Several PNACs had focused on ordering and manufacturing procedures that promoted flexibility. Customers could modify their orders in significant ways and still receive, within twenty-four hours, fresh products made on the same day. By comparison, in 1985, the average time delay between a product's manufacture and purchase date was about eight days. This delay was progressively reduced to a single day in more than 80 percent of cases. Hypermarket customers could find products on the shelves that were manufactured the day before, and BPG was the first in its market to show the manufacture dates on all its products, even though their only legal obligation was to mention the expiration date (Savall & Pasquier, 2012).

BPG's Agility

It is natural at this point in the BPG story to ask: "Is BPG an agile organization?" Agility is what allows an organization to respond in a more timely, effective, and sustained way than their competitors when changing circumstances require it. In other words, agility is repeatable. It is not something that happens accidentally or once; it is a deliberately cultivated dynamic capability. So with respect to the two standards of agility, the short answer to the question is "no," but BPG is well on its way.

The Outcomes Standard

The first standard of agility—the outcome standard—is a really tough test for most organizations, and BPG's experience at this point is too limited to yield an affirmative answer. The case clearly demonstrates that BPG had successfully changed and adapted. However, the organization has not yet demonstrated that it is adaptable. Adaptability means being able to change over and over again, not once or in small ways, but in adjustments that result in the development and implementation of new capabilities. So far, BPG has demonstrated that it has a robust freshness and quality strategy with strong ecological dimensions that has allowed it to grow. But other than adding a regional market, the strategy has not changed. Similarly, BPG added and organized its second site in a federation sort of way that did not require a major reorganization, and it has simply scaled up its operations, sales, and HR practices. This does not take away from the impressive results, but it has not changed multiple times or changed its capabilities. Similarly, while BPG's performance and performance improvements are admirable, at this stage of the company's and industry's life cycle, there simply isn't enough data to say whether their performance is "above average" and whether it has been above average for a long time.

The Organization Standard

The second standard concerns whether the organization possesses the strategies, structures, systems and processes to change and perform consistently. Following the initial horizontal and vertical interventions from 1984 to 1988, a second phase of work aimed at maintaining the progress already achieved and furthering BPG's development began in 1988. The intervention team worked with BPG's top management team on a semi-annual basis to focus on changing the way decisions were made, how the management tools were applied, and how strategic investments were analyzed. This gave BPG managers a more detailed and explicit understanding of their business. By the mid-1990s, BPG was able to state clearly the principles that were guiding the organization's development. The three strategic principles or family values were referred to as "fundamental" by the company leaders and provide a basis for assessing BPG's agility at this point.

The first basic principle or fundamental was the use of *decentralized sites*. Beginning in 1988 with the creation of the second site in eastern France, a clear policy emerged about making each site a legally operating, limited liability, or simplified joint stock company. To support this principle, the organization employed a supplementary principle they called "hierarchical proximity"—there should never be too many levels between top management and workers in the field.

"Between me, as holder of the company's vision, and the operator, there should be no more than five levels to keep everyone in direct contact [...] with the world and business life." (Pascal Pasquier, 2011)

The decentralization fundamental extended to a variety of functional choices as well. For example, there was only a very small human resource group in the headquarters location and no separate HR function in the sites. HR issues were expected to be a part of any manager's responsibility.

The second fundamental principle was the *balance between operational and functional responsibilities*. Each site was expected to sell and serve its regional market; geographically dispersed locations allowed production and consumption to be viewed as local and integrated. Locating sites near customers and sourcing ingredients locally reduced delivery times, a key aspect for ensuring the product's freshness, and kept its ecological footprint to a minimum.

High performance, according to this fundamental principle, and in the context of a distribution channel that demanded continuous price reductions and improved service, required seamless, daily coordination between production and sales. As a result, each site or subsidiary was largely self-contained, and one manager, from either marketing/sales or production, served as the primary leader but was expected to coordinate carefully with a deputy manager from the other function. Thus, a highly integrated duo composed of the two functions most critical to the site's success led the organization. A typical organization chart illustrates the balance between operational and functional responsibilities (Figure 2.8).

The third principle had the awkward label, the *synchronized strategic vision*. The purpose of the principle was to ensure that each site fully contributed to the strategy's implementation and its future development. The best example of this principle was BPG's development of a strategic vigilance process. By 1995, BPG executives had noticed a decline in both

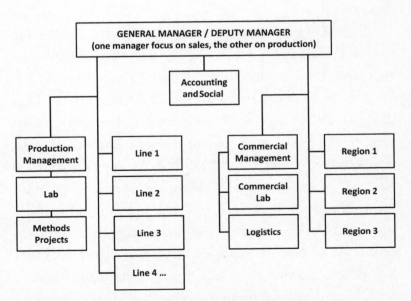

Figure 2.8 Typical BPG Site Organization Chart

process and product innovation. In response, it created "strategic focus groups" to explore medium- and long-term strategic issues, including new products, new markets, and changes in work processes. Focus groups at each site were chartered to monitor the evolution of a profession, a product concept, or a customer *for the company*. For instance, a manager at the Lyon site, which produced brioches, led a cross-functional, cross-site group to monitor social and economic issues related to brioche products for kids. His group was also responsible for proposing product development and marketing innovations. Proposals from these focus groups were validated by the executive committee and, as necessary and prudent, incorporated into the internal/external strategic action plan and site PAPs. Other companies would have placed these focus groups and responsibilities under a headquarters group. Instead, BPG decentralized the process to the site general managers and supported them with functional experts and middle managers.

These fundamentals suggest that BPG was well on its way to establishing agility routines, possessed a set of differentiated capabilities driving current performance, and were building a strong foundation of good management practices. That the organization had developed principles and fundamentals at all speaks to the emergence of change-friendly and robust strategizing routines. That BPG had developed a strategic vigilance process and flat structural arrangements speaks to the formation of a potential perceiving routine. That it has adjusted to strong customers and made changes in response to the SEAM implementation speaks to the development of testing and implementing routines. Finally, that the organization was growing and performing at rates that were satisfactory to the owners speaks to the quality of their differentiating capabilities. Thus, BPG had implemented some important changes but they had not, as yet, implemented any changes to their distinctive capabilities. Those capabilities—local sourcing, close customer relationships, decentralized operations management, and highly integrated, self-contained sites—were enhanced through the SEAM intervention, but have not changed at this point.

These fundamentals also make it clear that most of the work to date at BPG has focused on building stronger management practices and improving its social performance (working conditions, communication-coordination-cooperation, and strategy implementation). The horizontal intervention changed the organization's core planning, operations, and human capital processes. The vertical intervention changed the production system to increase efficiency and converted hidden costs into value-added activities. These changes have affected resource allocation, HR incentives, leadership development, and goal-setting practices. The strategic vigilance focus groups are an effective environmental scanning process.

Importantly, the SEAM process did not just improve BPG's management practices. It changed them in very fundamental ways. First, it improved the clock speed of the processes. At the site level, production lines and teams shifted from an annual cycle of goals, initiatives, and incentives to a semi-annual one. Second, it improved the flexibility of the processes. The PAPs were not just driven top-down but bottom-up by "mini-diagnostic" sessions that fed in local information to senior management thinking. Moreover, the PAPs and the PNACs meant that individuals, teams, and managers could contribute to current performance, future potential, and change.

Thus, while many of the changes developed during the SEAM implementation were contributing to all three layers of the Agility Pyramid—routines, capabilities, and management practices—agility is an advanced organization capability. The changes have not yet cumulated or been integrated together into repeatable routines of agility and consistently above average performance. We cannot say, at this point, that BPG is an agile organization. But all that is about to change.

References

Buono, A., and Savall, H. (2007). "SEAM in the context of merger and acquisition integration." In A. F. Buono and H. Savall (Eds.), *Socio-economic intervention in organizations. The intervener-researcher and the SEAM approach to organizational analysis*. Charlotte, NC: Information Age, 2007.

Galbraith, J. (2002). *Designing organizations*. San Francisco, CA: Jossey-Bass.

Pasquier, S., and Pasquier, P. (2012). L'entreprise généalogique: Réussir la transmission. In H. Savall and V. Zardet, *Les entreprises familiales: Création, gouvernance et succession*. Paris, France: Econimica.

Savall, H., and Pasquier, P. (2012). "Entrevista a Pascal Pasquier." *Revista Costos y Gestion, 86*, pp. 52–55.

Savall, H., and Zardet, V. (1987). *Maîtriser les coûts cachés*. Paris: Economica.

Savall, H., and Zardet, V. (2008). *Mastering hidden costs and socio-economic performance*. Charlotte, NC: Information Age.

Savall, H., and Zardet, V. (2011). *The qualimetrics approach: Observing the complex object.* Charlotte, NC: Information Age.

Savall, H., and Zardet, V. (2014). Action research and intervention research in the French landscape of organizational research: The case of ISEOR. *International Journal of Organizational Analysis*, 22(4), 551–572.

Savall, H., Zardet, V., and Bonnet, M. (2012). "Développer la croissance de l'entreprise par une démarche socio-économique endogène." In K. Richomme-Huet, G. Guieu, and G. Paché, *La démarche stratégique: Entreprendre et croître.* Aix-Marseille: Presses Universitaires de Provence, pp. 175–186.

3

The Brioche Pasquier
Group Goes Global

Serge Pasquier reflected positively on BPG's development. His management team and organization had developed and applied important new skills following the SEAM implementation. These skills had led to important changes in the sales and operations functions of the organization. As well, BPG's internal capabilities continued to mature with the use of SEAM's management tools, improvement processes, and strategic and political decisions. Perhaps most importantly, BPG was growing with new sites, product lines, and distribution channels and by identifying and converting hidden costs.

BPG's strong growth rates—between 20 to 30 percent per year—were due primarily to organic activity. Beginning in the late 1980s, BPG grew by adding production/sales sites throughout France. In keeping with its fundamentals and SEAM's principles, tools, and concepts, BPG developed a strong belief that no site should be more than about 300 people. However, Serge and his brother, Louis-Marie, believed that continued growth was going to require a mixed approach that combined internal development as well as growth through acquisitions.

In 1992, the company added a pastry product line by building a new pastry plant and by acquiring several small national pastry businesses. Entry into this second product line also brought a second and significant industrial distribution channel that included governments, hospitals, the military, and schools, because those were the primary channels for pastry products. The company used the additional channel to expand their marketing of brioche products. BPG added a third toasted bread product line in 2001 with the Spanish acquisition described below.

Yet, Serge believed these new skills and functional capabilities needed to be leveraged and extended.

By the early 2000s, BPG was structured into two geographical business units (Figure 3.1). The company had diversified into three product lines (brioche, pastry, and toasted bread) and had ten sites, eight of which were in France, one in Spain, and one in Italy, and it continued to reflect the fundamental of synchronized decentralization. For example, BPG asked particular site managers to take responsibility for negotiating general terms

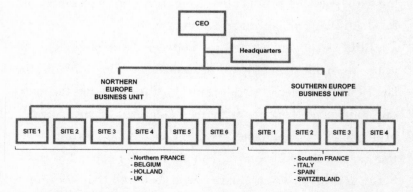

Figure 3.1 BPG Organizational Chart in early 2000s

and conditions with key accounts, such as Leclerc, Carrefour, or Auchan, for their product line as a whole. This strategic and political decision gave site managers an important level of responsibility that, in most organizations, would have been assigned to a headquarters national sales manager. The terms and conditions at the national level served a "pulling" function by establishing overall prices and product volume targets. In turn, each site and its sales team were responsible for "pushing" sales in the stores through promotions, events, and close relationships with store managers throughout the year. When the company only had one family of products, sales managers in charge of a key account negotiated for all the products and all the locations. This principle was initially retained when the diversification process began, but soon shifted to a product line specialization approach as distribution channel differences became clearer and international market demands became more complex.

Chapter Overview

At the end of Chapter 2, we argued that BPG could not yet be considered agile, despite significant and important organizational changes. We used the Agility Pyramid to explain that agile organizations are able to do what non-agile firms cannot: change the differentiating capabilities that allow them to deliver above average performance sustainably. At the top of the pyramid, the four routines of agility—strategizing, perceiving, testing, and implementing—described the processes necessary to change strategies and capabilities over time and stay in alignment with environmental demands. Surprisingly, though, it was a set of management practices—designed for both flexibility and speed—that supported the routines' effectiveness.

The SEAM process had clearly helped BPG in developing these flexible management practices, and the organization was building important, foundational characteristics. However, agility requires more than that. For all the change that had taken place in the service of growth, the organization had not built any new capabilities, but only extended and improved existing ones. To be agile, organizations need to meet the outcome standard of sustained above-average profitability and multiple changes, as well as the organization standard associated with the strategizing, perceiving, testing, and implementing routines.

This chapter extends the BPG story; it shows how BPG leveraged its flexible management practices to build strong agility routines. In particular, BPG changed its domestic capabilities into a set of international capabilities. This chapter describes the strategies and changes associated with internationalizing and globalizing the company.

BPG's growth and development into a global company proceeded in three phases or acts. Act 1, extending from about 1998 to 2000 (Figure 3.2), involved the internationalization of BPG's sales function. BPG extended its production capacity and sold brioche and pastry products manufactured in France to adjacent markets in Spain, Italy, Belgium, and other countries. By 2001, in Act 2, BPG began to take on additional risk (Figure 3.3). It invested in plant and equipment in different countries and changed its structure and operations. These adjustments represented small but important changes in its strategy—an increase in product line and market breadth, but relatively little change in the firm's aggressiveness and differentiators. In Act 3, BPG extended itself globally from the relatively simple operations associated with internationalization to the more complex operating issues associated with investments in firms outside Europe (Figure 3.4). Over a sixteen-year period,

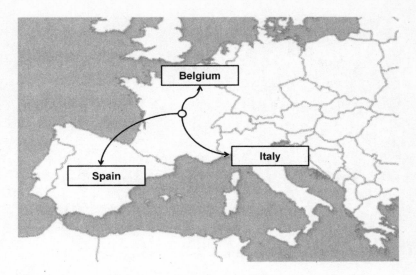

Figure 3.2 Act 1: Internationalizing the Sales Function (1998–2000)

BPG became more complex, changed many of its management practices and developed new capabilities, but it did not change its basic character and identity.

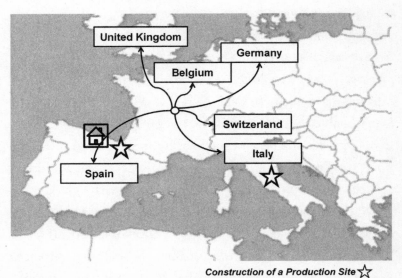

Figure 3.3 Act 2: Internationalizing Production (2001–2007)

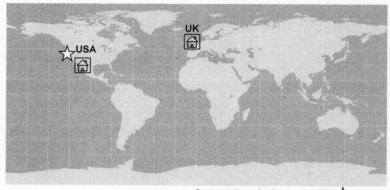

Construction of a Production Site ☆
Acquisition of a Production Site 🏠

Figure 3.4   Act 3: Globalizing Operations (2007–2014)

Act 1: Internationalizing the Sales Function

Following a logic that the case research has described well (Chandler, 1972; Rumelt, 1974), BPG saw the efficiency of their plants as a key resource to leverage for growth. *"In conversations with my brothers, we realized that brioche products easily could be consumed in other countries. We wondered why we could not participate and set off on this adventure."* Having captured a significant share of the brioche market in France, BPG thought it reasonable to move across the border. Because of increases in operating and sales efficiency owing to the SEAM interventions, the French manufacturing facilities possessed additional capacity that could be used to supply other nearby markets.

Such an approach supported the organization's basic strategy of local sourcing and local distribution, but also stretched the notion of local customers, since the delivery distances were increasing and would challenge the freshness component of the strategy. To mitigate those challenges, the first countries entered—Italy, Spain, and Belgium—were near existing production sites. In keeping with its strategy and decentralized approach, a site's sales director was given responsibility for these new markets.

BPG managers found the decision easy because each country possessed significant advantages, including French customers, French businesses and retailers, and a set of commercial relationships. BPG's arrival supported the European development of French businesses, and BPG supported this trend by establishing sales offices with French employees living locally in Spain, Italy, Germany, and Belgium.

The company believed that a French, but locally based, sales force would better understand the culture, its consumption habits, and its distribution and channel management requirements. BPG expatriated French salespeople to these countries and immersed them in the local markets. This proximity-based strategy—locally sourced products from nearby plants and expatriate salespeople—distinguished BPG from the typical competitor that hired independent commercial agents or leveraged a highly centralized sales force from its headquarters office.

BPG's initial international strategy was successful. It scaled up the SEAM-based management tools and strategic/political decisions as well as BPG's fundamentals. Products were supplied to new markets from existing sites, and expatriated BPG employees galvanized local sales in the foreign countries. Between 1998 and 2000, sales and net profits increased by 15 percent. This first step—a basic extension of the successful strategy in France—was mostly due to the robustness of BPG's strategy, BPG's national reputation, and its strongly shared purpose and fundamentals.

Act 2: From International Sales to International Production

Act 2 of BPG's globalization, between 2001 and 2007, began with the acquisition of two medium-sized companies, one in Spain and one in Italy. The common goal of both acquisitions was to establish international manufacturing sites and to learn to work with local employees. BPG's experiences in Act 1 sensitized it to the use of French expatriates. But as we will see, it required some learning to be competent at it.

The Recondo Acquisition in Spain

BPG acquired Recondo in 2001. Located in the Basque Country and only about a mile from the French border, many Recondo managers spoke Spanish and French fluently. Recondo was well known for their toasted bread "biscotte." This new product complemented BPG's traditional brioche and pastry products and expanded the product portfolio. However, there were important differences. The manufacturing process for toasted bread required a second cooking process and resulted in a longer "use by" date, but it also meant that the biscotte product line's margins were smaller. Brioche's more delicate structure and shorter "use by" date meant that delivery and restocking schedules for the two products were different and not aligned. Brioche products required more frequent store visits, and the differences in the manufacturing processes required increased plant capacity and production line scheduling coordination.

Complicating matters, Recondo's managing director left the company soon after the acquisition was complete. BPG's desire to keep the acquisition on track led executives to believe that sending a reliable French manager to Spain would best help the integration. In response, BPG expatriated a highly skilled, sales-oriented French site director to carry out the integration process and to run the Spanish site.

Unfortunately, the sales orientation of the French manager meant there was no "manufacturing" expertise at the top of the subsidiary. Thus, sales efforts to increase market share and to integrate the existing sales force into the BPG organization model received more attention. Such a focus also implied that the integration of the manufacturing teams and the important coordinating processes between them and the sales force were neglected. This slowed their integration into BPG's management system.

Although BPG kept most of the existing employees to maintain the site's stable functioning, many of the Spanish employees resisted its organization and management model. As the integration proceeded, it became clear that the source of this resistance was distrust in management. A common story among the workers described how "the former managing director was always leaving the light on in his office to pretend to the workers he was in the building." Other integration difficulties were a function of three languages in the Spanish subsidiary: French, Spanish, and Basque. Although managers were often bilingual, plant workers were less likely to speak Spanish, but only Basque. The evaluation phase of SEAM's improvement process suggested that the Spanish workforce saw the SEAM-based BPG management system as mostly "decreed." Spanish managers did not understand the philosophy behind these tools, only that they "had to be implemented." The integration process for this first Spanish site was difficult and painful for both the organizations.

Despite the integration difficulties and Spain's growing economic challenges, Recondo's performance improved. By

2004, a second site, less than one mile from the first one, was built to manufacture new kinds of toasted breads, and, in 2013, BPG decided to build a new production line to manufacture Brioche products. Total BPG staff in Spain grew to about 250 employees in 2014. Sales in the Spanish market reached about 67 million euro and consisted of products produced both in country (50 percent) and imported from French sites (50 percent).

The Brescia Acquisition in Italy

Also in 2001, BPG purchased Brescia, an Italian company that manufactured and marketed brioches and other similar products. As in Spain with Recondo, the integration of Brescia did not go smoothly. Many Brescia employees left the company a few months after the integration process began, often complaining of the mandates to follow the BPG management system. Another difficulty was the inability of the sales force to promote French products in the Italian market, where many large, well-established competitors were already operating. BPG eventually sold the subsidiary in 2006 at a loss of 4 million euros.

After five years of effort, the results from two forays into operating international subsidiaries were mixed. While BPG sold the Italian subsidiary at a significant loss, the Spanish subsidiary was performing well, despite the difficult integration process, a less profitable toasted bread market, and the country's poor economic context.

Common Difficulties in the Recondo and Brescia Acquisitions

ISEOR conducted an evaluation of BPG's efforts in Spain and Italy and developed three primary conclusions (Savall, 2014). First, BPG underestimated the necessary investment to market and work with different types of retailing networks. The Spain and Italy networks were structured and organized differently than the French networks. Despite the large concentration of French-speaking people and businesses in both countries, the local business networks in Spain and Italy were more "protectionist." Large, local, and well-established supermarkets with large market shares actively preferred Spanish and Italian suppliers. Moreover, many large retailers were not willing to support BPG's synchronized decentralization model by which one team negotiated high-level terms and conditions with tailoring of products and promotions at the local level. As a result, BPG was not able to ensure that the same product would be in all the stores and supermarkets of a given chain, and this led to an uneven presence in the market. Together, these issues created larger entry barriers and barriers to foreign companies than BPG had anticipated. The key and clear lesson was to be sure to understand the retailing networks in a country.

Second, the similarity between the high gastronomic preferences of the Spanish, the Italian, and the French cultures turned out to be more of a weakness than a strength. Despite all the benefits of such a culture, many Latins were not readily willing to try new products. The expectation of high quality tended to prevent experimentation with foods they were not familiar with. For example, if your preference in automobiles is Ferrari and Mercedes, you are not likely to try a Cadillac or Volvo, even though they are in the same class. A BPG manager observed: *"You can't make a Spaniard or an Italian eat anything you want!"*

Third, BPG lacked a nuanced understanding with regard to managing the internal organization and integration issues.

For example, BPG managers underestimated the power of human motivation and informal relationships. These forces could easily outweigh the legal and financial considerations of success (Buono & Savall, 2007). Some local Spanish and Italian employees left the subsidiaries a few months after the acquisitions took place. Others did not leave, but were very resistant to the organizational changes being implemented. BPG underestimated the high level of hidden costs related to high staff turnover and low productivity of these people. These costs were hidden insofar as they were not anticipated and measured in the acquisition financial package.[1] However, legal issues were also a problem. Labor law differences and contractual issues regarding human resource practices affected the integration process. Wage, bonus, and severance policy differences made it difficult to find common organizational practices to facilitate coordination between BPG and its acquisitions (Savall, 2014).

A site's geographic and psychic distance from headquarters also played a big part in the dysfunctions that occurred. Early in

---

[1] The reader might wonder, since ISEOR had been with BPG for years and knew about hidden costs, why were those principles not applied here? In fact, hidden costs had become a way of thinking about decisions since 1984. However, hidden costs had not been quantitatively measured since the late 1990s and ISEOR was not directly involved in the integration of Recondo and Brescia. At the time (2001), ISEOR had only begun thinking about maintenance interventions. The events at BPG actually brought out the idea that ISEOR should extend its services to include the design and implementing of "maintenance intervention programs." The objective of a maintenance program would be to sustain the good management practices of SEAM by engaging in some very practical activities, especially with new people in a client's company. This learning approach, not to put too fine a point on it, demonstrates ISEOR's agile capabilities. Today nine out of ten clients buy a maintenance program at the end of the first intervention.

the integration process, a top BPG manager with strong commercial expertise was expatriated to run the Spanish subsidiary. Another BPG manager was appointed to operate the Italian subsidiary and commuted from his home in France. Through the expat French manager and the commuting manager in Italy, BPG tried to impose its strong, family-based organizational culture on the Recondo and Brescia acquisitions. Although BPG's culture promotes values of openness, involvement, and engagement, there are a variety of implicit management and organization rules and policies that are not obvious to outsiders. For instance, although BPG's culture of inclusion did not reflect the broader French preference for hierarchy, the Recondo and Brescia cultures did. This clashed with BPG's culture, where being responsible for a team does not mean you make all the decisions. According to BPG's culture, each individual is a potential leader through priority action plans and periodically negotiable activity contracts. This expectation of individual-level empowerment and influence was not easily transferred to the new subsidiaries. Moreover, Spanish and Italian people were often intolerant of non-native speakers, and long-distance relationships between people speaking different languages made it doubly difficult to obtain the cohesion needed for success.

For BPG, Act 2 was equal parts pain and success.

"We should have paid more attention to the integration strategy we used in Spain and Italy. I made some mistakes in Spain because, intellectually speaking, while people understood the BPG system as part of a 'copy-paste' approach, they did not easily embrace it." (Director of Toasted Bread BU)

Still, the organization believed that international expansion was the right growth vehicle.

Recovering from Difficulties

BPG tried to learn from their Recondo and Brescia integration experiences and move the organization forward. In Spain, BPG appointed two local managers, one from sales and one from production, to lead the organization according to the fundamental principles. Together, they implemented a second wave of integration processes to help workers—especially those manufacturing teams that had worked under Recondo's old system—acclimate to the BPG organizational and management system. Eventually, the priority action planning and PNAC processes were adopted. In addition, an in-depth reorganization of the sales force, dropping the French sales model, allowed the Spanish sales force to sell different product lines (brioche, toasted bread, pastry), in contrast to the French sales teams that sold only one of them.

Recapturing the Italian market took longer and required a different business model. Following the sale of Brescia in 2006, a nephew of BPG's CEO spent eight years, from 2006 to 2013, developing a network of local Italian agents. It began with a partnership between BPG and two Italian sales agents to sell products sourced from an Eastern France BPG site under the "BP" brand name. During that time, sales increased in Italy faster than when BPG acquired Brescia in 2001. Fabrice Sciumbata (International Director of BPG) explained the advantage of this approach: "*In this model, BPG is able to keep the customer relationship central by including the sales agents in our biannual strategic meetings.*"

Act 3: From International to Global

Act 3 began with a CEO change in 2007, an issue that had come up as early as 1984 when BPG asked ISEOR to help them think about a successful transition to the next generation. Serge Pasquier, the industrial and financially oriented executive, and Louis-Marie, the top sales executive, were succeeded by their youngest brother, Pascal Pasquier. Pascal was a sales-oriented executive with twenty years of international experience.

Pascal recognized several challenges ahead. Given the French national context, he believed BPG's future growth would rely even more on internationalization. BPG's French market share had topped out at 45 percent, and gross margins were decreasing with market maturity. The national brioche market was not likely to grow, even with BPG's leadership. Moreover, pursuing further market share growth would be expensive and might require investments that were counter to the culture and fundamentals that had been cornerstones of the organization's success. For example, further growth in sales and market share in France might require changes to the decentralized fundamentals.

To position the organization for further internationalization, Pascal proposed and implemented a reorganization in 2007 (Figure 3.5). At the top, a group executive committee, including the CEO, the directors and deputy directors of the business units, and key functional managers from the headquarters staff, ensured overall company coordination. It made strategic decisions on investments and other organizational, industrial, commercial, financial, and human resources issues. Five functions—finance, human resources, legal, IT, and

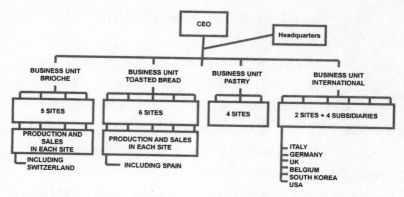

Figure 3.5 BPG Organizational Chart (2007)

technology development—representing fewer than 100 people reported to the CEO and constituted the headquarters organization. This headquarters unit had been kept deliberately small since the building of the second site in 1986 and the adoption of the "power of sites, lightness of headquarters" fundamental of synchronized decentralization.

Also reporting to the CEO were three product line–based business units (BUs) and an international BU. The brioche BU remained the largest force in the company, the second BU focused on the pastry product line, and the Recondo acquisition formed the nucleus of the third BU. The international business unit had two main goals: growing volume and increasing product gross margins. Export logistics and sales functions that had been controlled by the French sites in Acts 1 and 2 were transferred to the international business unit. It was also tasked with managing all foreign subsidiaries, except the two Spanish sites that were affiliated with the toasted bread BU. This structure would eventually control seventeen sites and four subsidiaries, 3,800 employees, and €618 million ($850 million) in revenue.

By 2009, the new CEO was embedded in his position and believed BPG's strategic and sales-driven passion for international business should be accelerated. He led the development of a new international internal/external strategic action plan based on three axes: "producing local," "developing international partnerships/alliances," and "spreading the management system." With these axes established, BPG executives believed that future growth and integration processes would proceed more smoothly. Pascal also made international development a strategic priority by increasing the goal of international sales to €145 million ($200 million) in 2013, or 23 percent of BPG's overall sales. However, the company retained its original policy of assigning a site sales manager to negotiate broad terms for key clients with locally oriented sales activities at each site. As part of the plan, BPG targeted the United Kingdom and the United States markets for one new manufacturing site in each market by 2014 to 2015.

United Kingdom (UK)

The UK story is a blend of Act 1 and Act 3 activities. BPG had established a UK sales office in 2001, and products for this market were supplied by the Northern France site. French sales managers were expatriated there to market BPG products. Unlike the Spain and Italy subsidiary experiences, there were no French retailers in the UK market, so BPG had little working knowledge of possible UK customers and its retailing network.

In fact, however, the retailing networks in the UK were well structured and organized, and after fourteen years living in the UK, the managing director understood the local market dynamics. This allowed BPG products to be quickly and easily seen and sold in all the UK markets. The UK director commented: "*as soon as our products are sold into Tesco or Marks & Spencer, you can find them in each and every store and area of the country the next day.*" In addition, British consumers had open attitudes regarding food. The London area was very cosmopolitan and diverse, and when consumers tasted something and liked it, they usually bought it again.

The United Kingdom business was an unqualified success. Its growth was exponential compared to the rest of Europe. In 2013, the UK market accounted for €36 million in sales, 90 percent of which came from brioche products.

Consequently, BPG acquired the land to build a manufacturing plant in late 2013. The criteria for this decision included the large potential increase in sales, the ability to adapt products to the UK consumers' and customers' habits, and that two French sites had production lines fully employed for manufacturing and supplying the UK stores with Brioche products.

United States (USA)

Three decisions influenced the choice to enter the American market. First, in 2006 and 2007, BPG acquired two small French enterprises that were already exporting products to the United States. Second, BPG's success in the UK emboldened executives to target the U.S. market. The sheer relative size of the American market and the "American dream" of many French companies to operate there supported the choice. Finally, there were many points in common between the United States and the UK. They had similar cultures and large cosmopolitan cities; well-structured retail industries with similar store "atmospheres"; and changing views of food that encouraged trying and tasting new flavors.

As it considered U.S. entry, and despite the similarities with the UK, BPG's managers accepted that they were unfamiliar with the U.S. culture, market, and retail network requirements. Although the internationalization process was intended to be ambitious, it also had to be cautious. Rushing into the strategy might lead to talent-oriented and financial mistakes that would cost more than a sensible integration. Time and money were the two most ambitious requirements of internationalization, and BPG did not want to sacrifice either one of them to succeed (Les Champions de l'Industrie, 1984). As a result, and in keeping with the alliance axis in the new international strategy, Pascal began looking for a reliable and effective local partner. BPG executives believed this approach would result in a speedier, more focused effort and less distraction of management attention and energy.

In 2009, BPG's top managers met for the first time with executives from Galaxy Desserts at New York City's Fancy Food Show. Galaxy Desserts (GD), founded in 1998 in Northern California, produced mostly "handcrafted" up-market French-inspired products, such as tarts and mousse cakes. There was little automation in the manufacturing process and 160 employees generated €20 million ($28 million) in sales. The two owners, a French industrialist and an American sales expert, worked to ensure sustained annual growth. They had a well-established sales force and strong management values that complemented the BPG philosophy.

The relationship began with an agreement to import BPG products into the United States (Figure 3.6). Between 2009

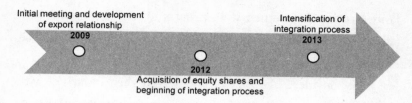

Figure 3.6 Chronology of BPG and the Galaxy Desserts Relationship

and 2012, both organizations worked hard to build a close and professional relationship, traveling to each other's facilities, making regular phone contact, and attending promotional events together: *"We have met them four or five times a year since 2009 and created a trustful relationship. Eventually, it led to us crossing the capitalistic stage."*

The "capitalistic stage" was crossed in January 2012 when BPG acquired 78 percent of GD's shares. GD became a BPG subsidiary and a careful integration process began. The two goals of the acquisition were to develop GD's existing business and brand name in the United States and to extend the brioche market under the French brand name "Brioche Pasquier." The first step was to test-market French products, extend its existing European-based supply chains, and learn how export, customs, and transportation costs affected pricing, margins, and product freshness. In addition, this slow integration process allowed BPG to reflect on the number of local staff (versus expats) required for success. Today, for example, the proportion of French staff in the United States is much smaller than in prior acquisitions and includes the CEO's nephew, who moved to California in January 2013. If the process went well, then BPG would consider building a new manufacturing plant.

Both organizations had to adapt their management practices and strategic activities. Although French and American executives worked well together, SEAM tools and processes had to be adjusted to function in the American environment. At the same time, French executives and middle managers continued to travel to California to increase their mutual understanding and find specific ways to progressively integrate the new subsidiary into the organization.

Summary

The initial SEAM implementation in France worked well because the process was formal, structured, and focused on key management practices. As BPG experienced "growing pains" associated with what one executive called the "copy-paste" model of acquisition integration, it became clear that a rigid mindset about a winning recipe prevented managers from deviating from that formula. As a result, BPG was slow to learn and adapt from their experiences, and there is some evidence that they strayed from the learnings of the original SEAM implementation. In fact, the rigid mindset was one of the biggest issues for BPG's managers.

Despite BPG's enlightened culture, the TFW virus can still operate—usually unconsciously—and managers must be mindful of its influence at all times. It is common for managers to fall back on old habits. French industrial experts and managers were critical of the foreign subsidiaries and the export team at the head office. Even though the strategy was widely shared and international development was a strategic priority, some BPG executives and employees struggled to adapt to new markets and cultures, but eventually learned and applied those learnings to its UK and U.S. experiences.

Assessing BPG's Agility

In prior chapters, we proposed two standards of agility. The outcome standard addresses sustained performance and change; the organization standard concerns the existence of agile routines.

BPG's Sustained Performance and Changes

The first standard of agility is outcomes-related. Can the organization demonstrate sustained profitability and capability changes? Even though BPG is a private company, its long relationship with ISEOR and access to financial databases provide us with a unique opportunity to assess its performance. First, as shown in Table 3.1, several economic and financial parameters show continuous improvement. Sales (turnover), profitability, employment, and productivity (sales/employee) all show significant growth over the twenty-seven years. Second, for twenty-one of those years, BPG was a public company on a regional exchange. During the period 1987 to 1997, the Boston Consulting Group ranked BPG first among European companies in generating value for its shareholders. Finally, since the 1980s, BPG has acquired and maintained its leadership position on the brioche market, has created jobs, and has implemented social innovations repeatedly hailed by the regional and national press.

A comparison of the company's financial performance relative to the industry is difficult over the long term, considering BPG's movement in and out of the equity market and the

Table 3.1 BPG's Business Indicators (1986–2013)

	Turnover (Sales in Millions USD)	Net Income (Millions USD)*	Employees	Productivity (Sales in thousands of USD/ employee)
1986	37	100	260	142.30
1990	103	535	604	170.53
2000	363	2853	1685	215.43
2002	479	2713	2444	195.99
2007	683	932	3000	227.67
2010	721	1613	3034	237.64
2012	808	1525	3171	254.81
2013	840	1851	3167	265.24
Growth rate 1986–2013 (27 years)	21.7 2170%	11.2 1120%	0.86 860%	1.51 151%
CAGR	12.26%	11.41%	8.5%	3.47%

*Net income figures indexed to 1986 = 100

fragmented nature of the industry. Table 3.2 presents a comparison of BPG's overall ROA and the ROA of its Brioche BU with a key competitor and the industry average over the last ten years. The data suggest that BPG's ROAs have consistently exceeded both competitor and overall industry average ROAs. For the nine-year period between 2004 and 2012, BPG's overall ROAs exceeded the industry average ROA 89 percent of the time (eight out of nine years). The Brioche BU's ROA was above a key competitor in that space 100 percent of the time between 2003 and 2013.

Table 3.2 Comparison of BPG ROAs with a Primary
Competitor and Industry Average

Years	Average BPG ROA*	Brioche BU ROA**	Main European Competitor ROA	Industry Average ROA***
2003		9.19	3.50	
2004	12.98	7.94	–4.25	6.83
2005	5.96	3.29	–0.73	6.04
2006	7.35	4.87	0.23	4.85
2007	6.25	2.26	–0.37	4.75
2008	11.02	4.16	0.31	3.53
2009	19.80	12.03	3.56	3.17
2010	10.04	8.00	1.35	3.55
2011	10.14	5.78	1.48	3.07
2012	14.10	7.78	0.70	2.54
2013	N/A	N/A	0.95	2.89

* The ROA for all the BPG subsidiaries averaged together

**The ROA for BPG's Brioche BU, which competes directly with the European company

***The average ROA for all EU organizations in the NAICS 3118 category

The second part of the outcome standard suggests that agile organizations are able to demonstrate multiple organization changes; the last two chapters have documented a wide variety of organization adaptations and initiatives. The toughest test is whether the organization can show changes in their differentiating capabilities.

At one level, Table 3.3 suggests that BPG's capability set changed from a producer and deliverer of a single product in a single country to a producer and deliverer of multiple products

Table 3.3 BPG's Capability Changes

Period Strategy	1974–1990 Build the Brand	2000–2007 Expand the Brand	2008–2014 Leverage the Operating Model
Capabilities	• Single, high-quality product/single channel • Single country distribution • Local source/local distribution • Close customer relations • Cohesive, participative, high-involvement culture • Efficient plant operations	• Multiple products/multiple channels • Single region distribution • Local source/local distribution/ coordinated sales • Understanding distribution and retail networks • European integration • Product and market creativity	• Multiple products/ multinational channels • Multiple regions • Local source/export distribution/ coordinated sales • Alliances/networks • Cross-cultural integration • Cross business units learning process
SEAM contributions	• Initial SEAM intervention and maintenance processes	• SEAM tools were used in formal and informal ways and applied in every site • SEAM principles/fundamentals were adapted to the new organizational configuration	• SEAM tools were used and applied in every subsidiary • Some SEAM/fundamentals were applied, some were not, in the case of one division and some subsidiaries

on a multinational basis. This large operating capability change was underpinned by various specific capabilities, including managing more complex production sites, managing more complex coordinating routines with the sales/delivery processes, understanding the structure/operations of different retail networks, making decisions with socio-economic criteria, and managing larger supply chains while maintaining freshness standards.

During the "Build the Brand" strategy between 1974 and 1990, what differentiated BPG in the marketplace was a fresh product paired with a strong, consistent, and locally responsive operation. The regular listening to customer needs led to a variety of innovative products and services, increased market share, and meant expansion into other parts of France. For example, as BPG tried to build its brand and image around a traditional, quality product, it had to address customer strategies aimed at boosting sales of store brands rather than producer brands. BPG's responsiveness proved to be effective in this regard. Between 1996 and 2001, while BPG produced product under store-brand names as well as its own "Brioche Pasquier" brand, it reduced the amount of production capacity dedicated to supermarket brands from 20 percent to 10 percent, while its total revenues rose 18 percent and the market shares of supermarket branded products fell by 34 percent. The evolution was a little different in the toasted bread BU, where supermarket brand shares were much higher. However, BPG's objective was to keep the proportion of revenues from its own brand as high as possible to support its identity and drive higher profitability.

As BPG internationalized, what eventually differentiated the organization was the creation of an aligned and cohesive culture, management system, and decision-making routine. It allowed local responsiveness to scale up globally. As product/ market and production technology breadth increased and scheduling and coordination became more complex, BPG's capabilities and operating models shifted from domestic to international to multinational and from simple to sophisticated. However, it was the alignment of the management approach and culture that drove success.

In the early phases of the organization's history, BPG had developed a high level of internal cohesion among its leadership team, site managers, and operational teams. This strong emotional bond was built thanks to a clear strategy, SEAM management tools, and the "values" of the company. It led to a solid strategic base that allowed BPG to adapt to a variety of environmental challenges. For example, this shared point of view allowed BPG to make innovative industrial and commercial choices compared to its competitors and compared to mainstream business models. Unlike its competitors, who outsourced distribution activities, BPG kept an integrated logistics function. It reinforced the freshness brand promise and enabled reliably fast delivery to the clients. In a market with extremely fierce price competition, where consumers expect constant price decreases, their cohesive approach maintained profitability through an efficient and effective periodic recycling of its hidden costs into value-added activities. The PNACs routinely identified these hidden costs and rewarded employees for innovative solutions.

This cohesion also facilitated strong lateral connections at different levels. For example, cohesion improved production and sales coordination at the site level and between the enterprise level internal/external strategic action plan and local priority action plans. It brought operational and functional staffs closer together in the plants, the commercial teams, the sites, and the head office. Finally, alignment led to maintenance and quality representation in the production line teams and encouraged coordination in the priority action plans and PNACs.

When BPG started operating internationally, this alignment and cohesion was both a strength and a weakness. It provided clear operating principles and recipes for sales functions and operating teams at new sites, but applying it in a "copy-paste" model was a weakness. It was not until the Galaxy Desserts experience that the organization demonstrated the lessons learned. Today, BPG operates with a mixed model that prizes the values of the company, but customizes some practices.

This consistent but adaptable approach is reflected in the development of decision-making capabilities based on socioeconomic rather than simply short-term financial criteria. After the initial SEAM implementation, BPG appeared to forget and remember these decision-making lessons several times. They were formally learned during the first SEAM implementation when strategic priorities in the business plans were broken down into the site's priority action plans. Importantly, these decisions found their way into individual and team-based PNACs and were connected to rewards.

After this initial implementation and as the organization grew internationally, this decision-making rationale often became informal. The organization's decision to realign the sales force across product lines in Spain is a good example. After the integration process was restarted, they used the concept of hidden costs informally to support the decision to deviate from the product line sales-oriented model. But using hidden costs also remained a formal capability. For example, in the 1990s, BPG used an analysis of hidden costs to augment the traditional financial analysis of discounted cash flow when it bought a small manufacturer of brioche near an existing plant. The question was whether the two sites should specialize in different products or each be a multiproduct site. The integrated analysis supported the decision to create, within the brioche BU, two multiproduct and self-contained sites, even though they were near each other. The decision also confirmed the importance of the decentralized site and balanced functional fundamental principles.

There is good evidence at this point to say that BPG has met the first standard. They have demonstrated consistently above-average performance over a long period and have implemented important, substantive changes in their differentiating capabilities.

BPG's Agile Routines

The second standard of agility is organizational. It answers the question, "How was BPG able to maintain its performance and make the capability changes described above?" A review of BPG's activities—especially its implementation of an international strategy—supports the conclusion that the organization is now in control of the strategizing, perceiving, testing, and implementing routines.

Strategizing

This routine reflects the way executives define purpose and strategy and how they promote an empowering social climate in the organization. First, agile organizations don't define strategy like other firms. For them, it involves a sense of *shared purpose*, a stable but change-friendly *identity*, and a robust strategic *intent* that clarifies how the firm will tactically differentiate itself in the current marketplace. Traditional organizations tend to have espoused values and purposes that are disconnected from the reality of organization members. There is no integrated view of the central, enduring, and differentiated reasons for their success (Whetten, 2006) or they embrace outdated notions of competitive advantage.

One of the strongest justifications for BPG's agility and the strategizing routine is the emergence and influence of a stable but change-friendly identity and shared purpose. From its inception, BPG executives established, communicated, and reinforced a set of values and beliefs that deviated from the traditional French organization and a set of fundamentals that guided the organization's strategic and political choices over time. Although never referred to as an "identity," the organization has been consistent in the *way* it operates internally and the *way* it engages with the marketplace.

BPG's identity was initially formed and revealed by its choice to focus on product freshness, local sources, and customer responsiveness. These are the keys to understanding BPG's identity, because in many ways they have not changed and remain core to BPG's success. Its identity was reinforced by its choice to utilize the SEAM approach, and it became more formal and explicit with its codification of the fundamentals—decentralized sites/proximity, balanced/integrated sales and production, and synchronized vision. The consistent evolution and formalization of these values and fundamental principles parallels the evolution of BPG's image, brand, and reputation. BPG's brand promise of product freshness and its ability to work closely and carefully with its customers were the central ingredients to its reputation. Over time, the consistency of this behavior no doubt led to reputational and image benefits.

Originally coined during the codification of the company's fundamentals, the "power of the sites, lightness of HQ" motto refers to the criticality of a local perspective that has never changed. Even in the United States, it started with an alliance and let Galaxy's local knowledge drive the integration. It was a lesson learned from the Italy and Spain experiences.

However, the emergence of an identity is only the beginning. It must also guide change and decision making. In that regard, BPG pursued a series of strategic intents or "momentary advantages" that we labeled "building the brand," "expanding the brand," and "leveraging the model globally" (Table 3.3). Each of these intents and momentary advantages required a different set of capabilities, and the development of both strategies and capabilities were guided, explicitly and implicitly, by BPG's identity. The initial "building the brand" intent was about the establishment of a local orientation and the use of the synchronized decentralization principle to settle in and dominate a local region. When BPG went outside the French borders, it began to "expand the brand" using a similar formula in different countries. This strategy had mixed success. Whenever BPG deviated from its ideology, the organization experienced difficulties. When it tried to impose its management system in Spain and Italy, the integration stalled. As the organization learned, it led to the "leverage the model" strategy (one of the axes in the international strategic action plan) in different countries and regions. In each phase of growth, it was the power of sites and the lightness of HQ that guided initiative generation, project execution, and success.

Second, BPG executives set the climate for continuous change, for challenging the status quo, and for encouraging debate. The voice of the sites is maintained by keeping the HQ role small and giving the site managers responsibility for goal setting and accountability for coordinating marketing and sales. An interesting artifact of this climate is the very labeling of the planning process. The organization doesn't engage in the development of a "strategic plan," but works to produce a rolling, three-year "internal/external" strategy. In addition, the priority action plan and PNACs conceived at the local level provide a structure for strategic debates among top executives, middle managers, and the workforce.

Perceiving

This routine is about organizing to understand the short- and long-term context within which the organization operates. Agile companies take special care to accurately sense and communicate what is going on in the environment, including short-term shifts and long-term trends. The indicators of an effective perceiving routine include a flat structure that is tightly linked to its business environment, an effective future scenario process, open channels of vertical communication, and transparent business, operational, financial, and competitive information.

Organization structure plays an important role in the perceiving routine. Structures with a "maximum surface area" connect as many people as possible to different aspects of the environment. BPG's fundamental principle of self-contained sites and decentralized operations—manifest as local sourcing, local distribution, and local customers—ensured a high level of connection between the organization and its key stakeholders.

Because the maximum surface area characteristic is agnostic to the structural form, it does not matter whether the structure is functional, geographic, or divisional. BPG used all three. The key issue is contact with the environment so that people can sense environmental change. But sensing without communicating is wasteful, and communicating without interpreting is just noise. BPG's integrated planning process ensures that the information at the bottom is coordinated with perceptions at the top.

The SEAM-based planning process was transparent and facilitated the rapid movement of information. It represented an important "bottoms-up" and "top-down" communication channel. The integrated planning process—involving internal/external strategic action plans, PAPs, and PNACs—ensured that strategic direction was communicated downward and that dysfunctions were identified locally and communicated upward. Moreover, sales representatives were responsible for collecting and providing feedback on their customers, consumers, and competitors' behaviors.

In addition to short-term connections and adjustments, many of the good management practices started by BPG founders or added during the initial SEAM interventions have evolved and grown into a viable long-term scanning process. The strategic focus groups initially created in 1995 to scan different aspects of the environment and provide strategic intelligence were expanded to be a source of proposals for the group executive committee. The groups were also asked to pay particular attention to the orchestrated implementation of those decisions. They eventually converted themselves into the permanent strategic focus groups to maintain a constant vigil on environmental change and represent a source of cooperation to stimulate innovation.

Today, about twenty focus groups operate in the company, categorized by products, markets (retailing, catering), and core functions (e.g., research and development, technology, and human resources). It is a shared accountability where a site manager leads a cross-functional group composed of BU functional experts and associate executives from other sites or BUs. Far from being a waste of time and money, this organizational choice allows BPG to better interpret weak signals from the company's environment concerning competitors, current or future clients and consumers, and national and international legislation. It allows them to turn awareness of new norms, standards, and regulations into new products, processes, and other innovations.

This is an important feature. Many companies have scenario processes, but agile organizations integrate them with decision making on a routine basis. In similar-sized and larger companies, a specialized headquarters team usually conducts environmental scanning and strategic thinking activities, but rarely speaks to senior management. BPG's choice was motivated by the desire of the top management team to develop an in-depth strategic analysis grounded in reality and to encourage and reward multi-skilling in the plants.

Testing

More important than innovation alone is testing—the setting up, running, and learning from experiments to vet new products, capabilities, systems, processes, or businesses. Agile organizations test and refine their insights from the perceiving process with a broad range of relatively low-cost experiments. Effective testing and innovation activities at

BPG included gathering further intelligence through the vigilance groups, trying out new ideas on a smaller scale in the PNACs, or launching full-scale product development programs, as in the acquisition of the toasted bread product company in Spain.

The BPG case is full of these tests. For example, BPG tried out different risk models by initially opening sales offices in adjacent countries, acquiring firms in nearby countries, and going overseas. Along the way, BPG learned about cultural integration and management issues, differences in retail networks, and production scheduling and coordination processes. These learnings were scaled up to the UK and U.S./Galaxy Dessert experiences. In addition to promoting a connection with the environment, BPG's maximum surface area structure also encouraged testing partnerships. It routinely partners with suppliers and customers to think about new products, information flows, logistics flows, or research and development. For example, the company partnered with a supplier to experiment with Internet ordering to increase the data security and gain speed and efficiency. Another example is a joint project group with a client on the marketing and merchandising of fresh pastry (Pasquier & Pasquier, 2012).

BPG encouraged innovation, but also tolerated a good deal of the right kinds of failure. The difficulties in Spain and Italy were used as learnings, not as reasons to stop the internationalization process.

To support this testing and learning approach, agile organizations consciously build organizational slack in the right places. They hire people, spend money, and allocate time that may not contribute directly to the bottom line, but allows the organization to deploy resources rapidly against opportunities that may or may not pay off in the short run, without jeopardizing day-to-day operations. The best example of this is the periodically negotiated activity contracts. This socio-economic tool was a part of the larger planning process. PNACs not only created a continuous improvement process that supported existing strategy developments, but they deliberately encouraged and rewarded employees for creating future potential, using slack resources to try things out, and converting hidden costs into value-added activity.

Implementing

This routine represents an important bridge between the other agility routines and good management practices. It is responsible for the execution of the current strategy as well as orchestrating the implementation of new capabilities and strategies. No organization can rightfully claim to be agile unless it can demonstrate the ability to carry out change. As part of the outcome standard, agile companies have histories of successful transformations, restructurings, and merger integrations, and they excel at the execution of new product rollouts, policy changes, and compliance mandates. The earlier description of capability change supports the claim that an implementing routine exists. A telling feature of agile organizations, BPG's change capability is not relegated to a staff function at headquarters; it is embedded in the organization's planning process.

The common operational and strategic planning process is a major contributor to BPG's sustained performance over the last forty years. Formalized during the SEAM implementation, this system has been responsible for adjusting and adapting

BPG's site organizations to new environments and strategies because it builds new skills, provides a flexible architecture that supports continued operations, and embraces change and learning to improve. First, the planning process ensures that managers and employees develop new skills and knowledge. The PNACs set operational goals but also developmental goals that support the creation of potential, including new skills. In addition, the socio-economic competency grid tool lays out both existing skills and the kinds of competencies to be developed.

Second, the planning process provides an important architecture for changing. The rolling three-to-five-year internal/external strategic action plan keeps one eye on the future through its connection with the strategic vigilance focus groups. The priority action plans provide the energy and ability to break down a strategic idea into operational implementation activities in each site or department. Indeed, every six months, the process generates, includes, and implements new ideas, new objectives, and new projects in the PAPs and PNACs. Different business unit and site directors have short-term economic and financial objectives (for example, EBITDA, revenue, and yield on investments) as well as medium- and long-term ones. Annual negotiations on these economic objectives take place at the business unit and site levels. Then, economic and financial objectives are translated into decisions and actions by the business unit and sites directors. Finally, the organization has embraced change and learning. The planning process has evolved and changes through feedback, the identification of dysfunctions and hidden costs, and the conversion of those dysfunctions into value-added improvements.

Summary

BPG has demonstrated the ability to maintain performance and change. It has developed and been guided by a change-friendly identity, a robust strategy, and agile routines that support changing and learning. ISEOR's SEAM methodology was a central part of BPG's evolution. Organization development interventions, like SEAM, provide an important set of tools for helping organizations become agile.

References

Buono, A. and Savall, H. (2007). *Socio-economic intervention in organizations: The intervener-researcher and the SEAM approach to organizational analysis*. Charlotte, NC: Information Age.

Chandler, A. (1974). *Strategy and structure*. Cambridge, MA: MIT Press.

Les Champions de l'Industrie. (1984). *Classement des entreprises*. L'Usine Nouvelle, n 2475, 10/20.

Pasquier, S., and Pasquier, P. (2012). In H. Savall and V. Zardet (Eds.), V. *L'entreprise généalogique, transmission, entrepreneuriat et succession*. Paris: Economica.

Rumelt, R. (1974). *Strategy, structure and economic performance*. Boston, MA: Harvard University Press.

Savall, A. (2014). Endogenous factors for sustainable performance of family firms' internationalization process. Dissertation for doctorate in management sciences, CNAM, Paris.

Whetten, D. (2006). "Albert and Whetten revisited: Strengthening the concept of organizational identity." *Journal of Management Inquiry, 15*(3), 219–234.

4

Implementing Agility and SEAM

Recommendations and Implications

Brioche Pasquier Group's (BPG) journey to agility is a story of patient success. Over a forty-year period, the implementation of a socio-economic approach to management (SEAM) resulted in flexible management practices that BPG leveraged into routines of agility. This chapter places these specific BPG activities into a broader organization development context and highlights recommendations and lessons learned.

A Comparison and Integration of Agility and SEAM

SEAM and agility represent complementary perspectives on organization change and effectiveness, but they are not the same thing (Table 4.1). In particular, the two models have

Table 4.1 Comparing Agility and SEAM

Dimension	Agility	SEAM
Focus	Design What	Change and learning How
Outcomes	Sustained Profitability	Sustained socio-economic performance
Intervention Strategy	No clear intervention strategy, only broad categories related to agility pyramid	Clear intervention strategy–transform "hidden costs" into value-added activities and activate human potential through socio-economic management tools and processes
Key Features	Agility routines	Strategic/political decisions
	Differentiated capabilities	Improvement process
	Good management practices	Socio-economic tools

distinctly different foci. Agility is an organization design framework that describes the kind of strategies, structures, systems, and processes required to generate sustained profitability. Its focus is on the features—routines, capabilities, and management practices—that allow an organization to make timely, effective, and sustained change. It views change, not stability, as the key to organization effectiveness.

The focus of the SEAM approach—combating the TFW virus by converting dysfunctions and hidden costs into productive activity and human potential—is about changing an organization. It seeks to replace obsolete assumptions about organizing with more sustainable ones, but it does not specify the strategic and political decisions an organization should make. Rather, it assumes that strategic decisions are not decisions *per se* but the outcomes of an ongoing negotiation process among the various stakeholders of an organization. The arrangement of socio-economic management tools, strategic/political choices, and improvement processes might result in an organization that can make timely, effective, and sustained change, but that was not SEAM's purpose. In BPG, the issue was how to use the SEAM approach to prevent the creep of the TFW virus into the organization. The Pasquier family did not want the organization to grow into a typical large bureaucracy.

As a result of this difference, the agility framework has no specific intervention strategy or intervention tools. At best, the Agility Pyramid provides broad categories of change activity. When applied to large, well-established firms, the methods of organization transformation may work well *if* they are implemented with an eye toward agility. That is, a top-down transformation process would have to be conducted with the explicit vision of creating a highly egalitarian and empowered culture. There are ironies and contradictions that would have to be addressed. In most cases, however, the typical, linear change management models used to guide such transformations tend to focus on narrow and specific changes, such as deploying new information technology systems, or broad organization initiatives, such as becoming more customer-centric. Based in project management, traditional models suggest that change will be over and leave the organization without the capacity to change again.

These general prescriptions for change are similar to SEAM's improvement process. SEAM's linear and disciplined approach is an appropriate change process for firms with the TFW virus because it is structured and controlled. However, its application at the organization level, its focus on dysfunctions and hidden costs, its objective of socio-economic outcomes, and its integrated use of specific socio-economic management tools distinguish the approach. SEAM's improvement process is not just a change management process, but a systemic change process.

Beyond those important differences, however, there are a number of complementary perspectives. First, both models are interested in similar outcomes. Agile organizations are able to post consistently above-average profitability; the SEAM intervention transforms organizations that can be more sustainably effective along social and economic dimensions. Second, both models represent normative frameworks using organization design features, tools, and change as core variables. SEAM is driven by a belief that the TFW virus's assumptions about people are inadequate for today's world, but it is not a "cookie cutter" approach and recognizes that each change journey will be a function of the organization's history, industry, culture, and strengths.

Similarly, agility is driven by a belief that sustained success in today's environment requires an embedded philosophy about the centrality and importance of changing. Finally, the two approaches have complementary views regarding top management's role in setting an appropriate climate for involvement in developing appropriate strategies. The agility framework, for example, is clearer about the characteristics of SEAM's internal-external strategic plan, while the SEAM methodology is more prescriptive about how management should behave in establishing a participative climate. In sum, although SEAM was not intended to implement agile organizations, it can be viewed as a specific process for helping organizations to become agile.

An Agility Implementation Framework

BPG's development arc over four decades—from its founding in 1974 to its emergence as a multi-national baking company in 2013—provides an opportunity to think about and describe the implementation of agility, to extract principles that other young organizations can follow. The BPG case is unique and informative because it was not a transformation of necessity. No performance crisis or technological disruption forced it to change, and no one in 1984, 1995, or 2001 said, "I think we should be agile." Becoming agile is an organization development process with important milestones.

The recommended organization development sequence below draws on the BPG case, ISEOR's extensive history of SEAM implementations, and our agility research case studies. It integrates the Agility Pyramid and the SEAM approach. We use the categories of good management practices and differentiating capabilities from the Agility Pyramid to represent the strategic and political decisions from the SEAM methodology, leverage many of the socio-economic tools, and accept the improvement process as an adequate framework for viewing organization life. The four routines of agility remain the core of the organizational standard.

As a result, and based on a sound diagnosis and analysis of an organization's current strengths and dysfunctions, young, growing organizations that want to emerge as agile should address three broad categories of change in roughly this sequence:

1. Strategize first
2. Lay the foundation
3. Lead the development of agile routines.

Developmentally, and the BPG case supports this observation, agile organizations are built on a foundation of good management practices and processes that are designed to support a higher level of functioning than those found in traditional organizations. These practices and processes deliver objectivity, transparency, timeliness, flexibility, and accountability so that decisions are consistently based on relevant facts. This is not as easy as it sounds, and such practices are rarer than you might think.

Even after years of initiatives and change, the managers at BPG and every agile organization we have worked with say the same thing: "We still have so much to learn." That is because the proof of agility is in the outcome standard, not in some management writer's use of a specific practice as evidence of agility. An organization with a good innovation process or with effective and agile leaders or a "flexible resource allocation system" is not an agile organization. Being agile means having all those things and above-average profitability more than 80 percent of the time for a long period; it means you have implemented a variety of significant changes and not lost a beat. It can be done, and it requires a steady hand. However, these good management practices require a context. The implementation of agility depends on a clear strategy.

Strategize First

Organization performance is mostly a function of strategy—identity and intent. Short-term performance derives from the quality of the strategic intent even more than its implementation. AT&T, the American telecommunications company, is routinely listed among the most inconsistent providers of coverage, quality, and customer service, yet profitability is strong because Apple gave it years of exclusive access to the iPhone. Long-term performance, on the other hand, derives from the organization's identity.

However, the strategizing routine involves more than specifying strategy. It requires creating a climate of openness and candor regarding strategy's renewal (O'Toole & Bennis, 2009). Developing a clear and shared strategy that is also encouraged to change by the organization's identity provides the context for designing good management practices and the transparency required for the other agility routines.

As described in Chapter 1, strategy is a wasting asset, and young organizations need to get off on the right foot. A strategic intent must be good enough to drive decisions about management processes, structures, and systems, and it must be robust enough to perform under a moderate range of environmental demands. This requires a clear understanding of the capabilities necessary for success and knowledge of where hidden costs may hinder progress. Young organizations can over-invest in making their strategic intents perfect or impossible to imitate. As a result, people may resist changes to commitments and tailored solutions that have proven successful, even in the face of tremendous pressures for transformation. They also may be reluctant to address hidden costs that appear to be unrelated to the strategy, but might lead to meaningful changes.

BPG's strategy was refined early in its evolution. Credit for a crisp strategic intent must go to the Pasquier family. Their insight and commitment resulted in an economic logic that minimized costs through local sourcing and local delivery, differentiators of product freshness and strong local customer relationships, and a narrow focus on brioche products and specific geographic markets. Despite high levels of buyer power, intense rivalry from both large, well-established firms and small local boulangeries, and changing regulatory requirements, BPG adapted in incremental and substantial ways. Over time, it used its understanding of the sales and production processes to increase product and market breadth, remain consistent but not aggressive (a point we will return to later), and press its differentiation advantage. A powerful and well-executed strategic intent was the single biggest driver of early performance.

But strategy is more than just a robust intent, and agility is more than adapting once. For organizations implementing agility, the development of a change-friendly identity is a much more difficult, much riskier, and much longer task to achieve. When the case concerns a young, growing, start-up organization like BPG, the challenge is to envision, encourage, and establish an identity that supports the evolution of robust strategic intents and signals the organization to not only expect changes to structure, capabilities, and other systems but to initiate them. The challenge for older, more established organizations is even greater. Managers in traditional organizations often quip, as Peter Drucker said, that "culture eats strategy for breakfast." In agile organizations, managers understand that it is identity's role to challenge the status quo and encourage change in strategy. Identity is the manifestation of the open and challenging context.

Identities, like culture, emerge over time and cannot be changed directly. It requires a serious and patient commitment on the part of the top management team to support organizational values, brands, and reputations that support change as the long-term key to success. It also requires that senior executives themselves commit to behaviors that align with these values and brand promises. There's no leeway for not "walking the talk" or not "doing what you say you will do." Management rhetoric about people being the most important asset or marketing slogans about superior customer service are easily sniffed out when the resources to back up such claims do not materialize.

As BPG made the transition from start-up to established firm, it sought the advice and assistance of ISEOR and learned about the philosophy of socio-economic performance. This philosophy aligned with family values; the importance of that alignment should not be understated. Our research on agility and sustainably managed organizations reinforces the importance of this alignment and identity (Mohrman & Worley, 2010; Worley, Feyerherm, & Knudsen, 2010). BPG's culture was not typically French. French organizations, like those in most other developed countries, tend to have formal hierarchical structures and cultures; the TFW virus has been embedded in them through years of history, regulation, and experience. The relative ease with which BPG adopted and applied the SEAM concepts is partly a function of the Pasquier family's non-traditional and empowering beliefs. But this development, roughly from 1984 to 1995, was not enough to make a claim of agility.

Symbolizing the complexity of establishing a change-friendly identity, much of the hard work is done in the next phase of implementation. Good management practices that increase flexibility and clock speed are the concrete systems that will support an identity's emergence. But establishing the context within which these good management practices will be built is of paramount long-term importance. The organization must continually reinforce the emergence of its new identity by applying what we call the "ITSS principle" (that is, "it's the system, stupid"). Managers must ensure that the design of every structure, management practice, or system supports flexibility and speed, the desired identity, and the other flexible and quick elements of organization design. A new incentive system cannot contradict the values or brand implied by the identity, and it must align with measurement systems and structures.

This is one of the biggest strengths of the SEAM approach. It contains not only a straightforward change process, but it also includes targets for change (strategy/political decisions or good management practices) and tools for managing. Consciously, and perhaps to some extent unconsciously, BPG used these tools to nurture the emergence of a change-friendly identity that was best captured by the motto, "power of sites, lightness of headquarters."

BPG's support of the "power of sites, lightness of headquarters" identity is a monument to the ITSS principle. The early years were about getting the strategic intent right and the family's commitment to assembling an organization design in support of that identity. They created self-contained sites, developed a planning system that involved the sites and their employees in material ways, incented people for both productive activities and the creation of potential, and empowered the sites through sales processes and strategic focus groups. These good management practices, changes, and decisions played a central and recurring role throughout BPG's development, but here they represent a concrete example of how organization design elements reinforced the emergence of a powerful identity.

Identity is central to the ongoing adaptation of an agile organization. Without a change-friendly identity, there is little likelihood of being able to make the changes necessary to sustain performance. That is, identity helps an organization challenge and change its fundamental business and management models without changing its essential nature. Maintaining the organization's identity even as it changes the dimensions of its strategic intent and organization design allows agile organizations to stay "exactly the same, only different." BPG in 2014 is not the same organization that it was in 1984, but in many ways, in ways that are related to its long-term success, it is exactly the same.

This characteristic dominated the internationalization process. Over and over again, BPG succeeded when it made decisions that gave power to the sites and local markets and stumbled when it tried to cling too tightly to a recipe or an HQ-dominated mindset. Success in Act 1 of BPG's internationalization accelerated when French sales agents were expatriated and immersed in the local markets. Along with locally sourced and fresh products, this differentiated BPG from the competition. In Act 2, the Spain and Italy acquisitions struggled with too much French oversight and a "cut-paste" integration plan, but prospered when integration processes went more slowly and the local organization was given the opportunity adjust in ways that fit the local circumstance. The entry into the U.S. market benefited from a patient alliance approach that culminated in an equity stake in Galaxy Desserts.

The power of sites, the lightness of headquarters is a long-term strategy, one that has not changed over forty years but encourages and expects change. While BPG's intent explains its performance at any particular time, BPG's identity explains why it has been successful over forty years. The key steps associated with Strategize First are shown in Table 4.2.

Table 4.2 Key Activities in the Strategize First Phase

Category	Comments and Activities
Clarify your strategic intent	• Specify and communicate the economic logic or business model. Everybody—top to bottom—needs to know how the organization makes money or delivers benefits to customers. Too many organizations believe "it's obvious" or "people will figure it out." It is not obvious, and it is management's responsibility to state this clearly. • In general, young organizations should have a narrow breadth (particular markets or products) and a few key differentiators. This simplicity helps diffuse the strategy and allows people to both succeed and learn. • Do not be overly aggressive. There is a time and place for taking on more risk, speed, and urgency. However, overly aggressive strategies, too early, risk making aggressiveness a part of the organization's identity and increasing the chances of mercurial performance. • Know what capabilities are needed and identify where hidden costs exist.

Clarify the values and brand promise that will define who you are as an organization	• IBM's former CEO Sam Palmisano said it best: "Values let you change everything, from your products to your strategies to your business model, but remain true to your essence, your basic mission and identity.... We wanted values that, like Watson's Basic Beliefs, would be enduring, that would guide the company through economic cycles and geopolitical shifts, that would transcend changes in products, technologies, employees, and leaders.... Values help you make.... decisions, not on an ad hoc basis, but in a way that is consistent with your culture and brand, with who you are as a company."
	• What is it that you want customers to experience? What promise will you make to them? Be sure the answers to these questions are realistic, connected to your intent, and supported with resources and management attention.
	• Heed the advice, "you only get one chance to make a good first impression." Have a clear plan to respond when you screw up. It will say more about your organization's identity than any marketing slogan.
Involve as many stakeholders as meaningfully possible in the above two activities	• Too many managers and executives have forgotten what we learned a long time ago. People are more likely to commit to a course of action when they are invited to participate in a decision that affects them.

Lay the Foundation

BPG's journey to agility was hastened because it first mastered the basic "blocking and tackling" of management. Too many young organizations adopt basic, traditional management processes out of expedience. They believe such systems do not require the same amount of attention as choices about technologies, products, and markets, and this casual approach opens the door to a variety of inefficiencies and hidden costs. They do not think about the long-term implications on identity, flexibility, or clock speed.

Similarly, organizations that adopt the latest management fad with the word "agile" attached to it do not understand the fundamentals of agility. Adopting agile software development, adaptive leadership, or lean manufacturing does not make the organization agile. Such an approach ignores the ITSS principle and the importance of the good management practices that are the foundation of the agile capability. Systems thinking, an important element of the ITSS principle, and appreciating the complex interplay among good management practices, such as setting goals, establishing effective structures, allocating resources, managing information flows, and designing incentives, separate effective management systems from ineffective ones.

At BPG, the socio-economic management tools were assembled into a planning and performance management system that supported freshness and responsiveness but were never locked around them. This is the key to flexibility. Like a robust strategic intent, the good management practices at BPG were able to function with inputs from the top, the bottom, or the outside-in. The systems were flexible by design. They easily adapted over time, even as they supported the efficient execution of any current strategic intent. The resulting set of practices represented the qualities and characteristics of good management practices at the bottom of the Agility Pyramid. Too often, resource allocation and planning systems fail because management measures the wrong things, fails to complete and restart the improvement process, or fails to design the systems with flexibility in mind. Moreover, BPG's planning and performance management systems were built around a six-month (as opposed to annual) cycle that supported its ability to adjust and adapt. The key activities associated with the Lay the Foundation phase are shown in Table 4.3.

Table 4.3   Key Activities in the Lay the Foundation Phase

Category	Comment and Activities
Use the strategic intent and intended identity as guidance to define the operational capabilities necessary for success.	For any particular practice—planning and budgeting, resource allocation, decision making, structure, coordination mechanisms, leadership development, rewards (monetary and non-monetary), environmental scanning, and so on—identify how the process will work over time, ensuring: • That the inputs to the system/process can vary in terms of sources and content categories. • That the process operates at a cycle time that allows for responsiveness to environmental demands. The cycle time—weekly, monthly, annually—will be a function of the industry and the particular system. • That the process is simple enough to be effective given the cycle time requirements. • That each management practice supports the other practices and the identity/intent.

Lead the Development of Agile Routines

Agile organizations know how to build and change capabilities as a matter of course. It is fundamental to the outcome standard. The responsibility to lead the development of these routines falls squarely on executives' shoulders.

Executives must understand that leading the building of capabilities or routines requires resources, organization systems and processes, and experience (Mohrman & Worley, 2009; Worley & Lawler, 2009). In that sense, many of the good management practices, such as resource allocation, performance management, or environmental scanning, are simple versions of capabilities. Good environmental scanning processes have skilled people, established stakeholder relationships, dedicated systems for gathering data, methods of analysis and presentation, and years of practice. The leadership challenge for organizations with a clear strategy and good management practices is to leverage and integrate these strategies and practices—over time—into agility routines. At BPG, the set of principles and beliefs, formalized as "fundamentals," complemented and guided the acquisition of new skills and resources, the evolution of its systems, and learning over time.

First, strategizing, perceiving, testing, and implementing routines depend on resources, especially skills and knowledge related to change. Although tangible resources, such as technology and physical capital, are important for any capability, they can often be easily acquired in different ways. However, change know-how can be quite specific, difficult to acquire, and hard to identify in advance. Subtle differences that can be critical are easy to overlook. Despite all the similarities between French and other Latin cultures, BPG did not see the differences in consumer behaviors, the importance of local manager influence, or how sales networks and product mix interacted in the initial Spain and Italy acquisitions. The operational capabilities did not function properly until leaders supported the development of this knowledge through an evaluation, and the perceiving, testing, and implementing routines did not emerge until BPG executives learned what it meant to change and adapt these capabilities in different contexts.

Second, building agility routines and changing capabilities requires an appropriate architecture to support the repeated application of these skills and resources. Executives must design and establish the structures, workflows, procedures, and systems to allow these resources to operate—to revise strategy, play with the future, or test and learn. Again, good management practices and flexible socio-economic management tools are critical. Without these infrastructural systems, there is no way to apply newly acquired skills and knowledge in a repeatable, systematic way. It is the features of these management practices—flexibility and speed—that permit the organization to implement one strategic intent, then transition to the next intent in response to environmental and marketplace changes, and yet maintain performance.

Finally, and perhaps most importantly, no capability as complex as an agility routine operates flawlessly the first time. It requires trials, failures, and eventual successes. That means leaders must be deliberate and patient. Executives must engineer the experiences and embrace the inefficiencies that result in learning how to perform the capability well. Over the course of the BPG case, the Pasquier family's experience, openness, involvement, and patience allowed the perceiving, testing, and implementing routines to develop.

Some of the skills and knowledge associated with a routine, such as flexibility and clock speed, can be learned through best practice and benchmarking exercises or through case studies and other publications. This is where SEAM's management tools, like the competency grid, performed well. It catalogued existing skills and, in light of future trends identified by the vigilance focus groups, helped managers know what skills to acquire or develop. Such an approach seems more powerful and superior to the traditional approach of forming validated competencies and training everyone in them. But in general, it is the actual operation of the good management practices that generate the data, information, and skills. BPG's understanding of other markets, retail networks, supply chains, and customer tastes—each an important element of perceiving, testing, and implementing—could only be learned through the experience of performing the good management practices or implementing a strategic intent.

Thus, experience and learning are at the heart of any capability change. If management has set a climate for openness as part of the Strategize First phase, the flexible and speedy features of good management practices are put to good use when the strategy changes. The first change in strategy is unlikely to be perfectly executed, and it is at this point in a young organization's life that identity emerges. How executives lead the change—with values and a brand promise at the center of the conversation—will inform the identity's label and support the development of agile routines.

BPG's first big strategy change was its entry into different country markets. Prior to this change, BPG's flat and decentralized structure, its strategic focus groups, and the planning process had operated somewhat independently. In opening offices and making acquisitions in other countries, a very different set of capabilities was required. BPG's progress occurred in fits and starts because it had to add skills and resources, develop or adapt existing systems, and learn. The organization encouraged and reinforced the power of sites and the relatively light touch of the headquarters organization by linking the scanning results of the focus groups to the planning process and keeping the process decentralized. The perceiving and testing routines emerged as BPG became better and better at applying the planning and vigilance systems at larger and larger operational scale. The bumpy but ultimately successful integration of the Spain and Italy organizations led to future strategic-level testing of alliance building and new plant construction in other countries.

Similarly, in developing local priority action plans and establishing periodically negotiable activity contracts, execution of the current strategy and potential future opportunities and capabilities were tested and implemented. The organization's patience, its ability to process information, and the clarity of its strategy and fundamentals were important contributors to the development of effective testing and implementing routines. Table 4.4 summarizes the key activities in the Lead the Development of Agile Routines phase.

Table 4.4 Activities in the Lead the Development of Agile Routines Phase

Helping the organization build the agile capability is ultimately a leadership challenge. With established values and an intended identity, top management teams must lead the learning process through five activities:

Categories	Comments and Activities
Staying consistent with the vision	Nearly every study of leadership points to the importance of a consistent message regarding the company's direction, including its strategy and values. The symbolic role of leadership—consistently communicating direction and backing up words with deeds—cannot be ignored.
Helping organization members "make sense" of events	The emergence of an agile capability is not a sure thing. It is fraught with uncertainty and unexpected events. As events and decisions are made, senior managers must help people see how the events are connected and how progress is being made. "Meaning making" is a critical role of top management.
Funding initiatives	There's an old saying, "it's better to ask forgiveness than permission." This recommendation suggests that executives need to get "out front" of the agile capability's emergence and proactively charter and sanction the initiatives that will make the most visible short- and long-term contributions to agility.

Looking for teachable moments to reinforce the new employment contract	People in an organization have diverse needs, motivations, and backgrounds. Executives must find people doing things right and visibly encourage the right kinds of behaviors. By the same token, if executives see the wrong kind of behavior, it is equally important to clearly indicate that such behavior is unacceptable and reinforce the values consistent with the desired identity.
Creating a space for dialogue	The most important leadership behavior—in keeping with the transparency required by the four agility routines—is to create time and opportunity for people to talk about the different initiatives and the extent to which agility is emerging. Executives need to lead the "are we heading in the right direction" conversation. Most executives shy away from this recommendation, believing that pulling people together to talk about change and design will only result in complaints and finger-pointing. But like an unhappy customer giving feedback, the information is vital to knowing how the implementation is proceeding and how best to make course corrections. It is an important ingredient in building trust.

Reflections on Becoming Agile

Young, growing, small-to-medium-sized firms have a great opportunity to make agility an embedded feature of their organizations and to make sustained, above-average profitability a habit. The deliberate pursuit of the agile capability can make change and changing a part of the organization's DNA.

This concluding section explores two implications of the BPG case. First, we look at the powerful and multi-faceted but enigmatic concept of hidden costs. It challenges many assumptions of a broken economic model and offers a new way of thinking about organization design and change. In combination with the agility concept, viewing the idea of hidden costs as an adjunct to strategic thinking can unleash a wave of innovation and change. Second, we explore the assumptions of aggressive growth and its relationship to sustained performance. The BPG case, along almost any dimension, is a big success. But it is one of patient success and wisdom that challenges traditional notions of leadership and growth.

The Power of the Hidden Cost Concept

BPG's turn away from bureaucracy and toward agility arguably began with the initial SEAM implementation. The hidden costs identified in the diagnostic phase suggested that the TFW virus was taking root and confirmed the fears of the Pasquier family. The results of more than 1,300 SEAM application cases testify to the centrality of stability assumptions and the TFW virus in most organizations. However, the genesis and implications of hidden costs—that traditional principles of organizing are misguided, distract managers from making effective decisions, and result in excessive expenses and opportunity costs that are not readily visible in financial statements—are difficult to explain and powerful in implication.

Converting hidden costs into value-added activity achieves the real effectiveness touted by the efficiency approach, but requires a deep rethinking of the business from the ground up. The diagnostic phase of a SEAM intervention not only paves the way for the project phase, but it represents the beginning of an important "rewiring" of the management brain. We used the story of the little Dutch boy to symbolize the issue. Most organizations set up (ultimately unnecessary) systems to plug holes in the dike instead of fixing the dike. Under the influence of the TFW virus, everyone knows how to plug holes well. Over time, the process is seen as normal. When the senselessness of this realization hits a manager's awareness, it is profound. It suggests that much of a manager's prior learning and experience has been focused on learning to hide inefficiency with elaborate systems; that such behavior was considered more valuable than preventive actions and proactive management. The concept of hidden costs thus challenges the way executives and managers see themselves, their business, and their industry.

The calculation of hidden costs and the learning that results from effective feedback processes helps managers and employees discover that their way of economic reasoning is ill-suited to today's world. It not only results in the identification of actions that create more value added in the short run, but it also turns managers away from a TFW distorted way of thinking. It opens their minds to agile reasoning.

However, the initiation of a formal and informal re-education of organization members, from top brass to individual contributors, must be systematic. The hidden costs concept is powerful because it introduces change gradually and progressively builds managerial capability. By initiating a SEAM process, the first objective is to reduce dysfunctional practices, an objective that can appear very hard for managers at the beginning. With patience, and when the first improvements are achieved, another step is possible. This progression over time allows managers and executives to renew the corporation's interest in strategic and innovative ambition.

For example, at BPG, the average period between producing and selling products in 1984 was about seven days. This situation produced high hidden costs because, as the product ages, consumption and the revenues that go with it decrease. BPG wanted to reduce that period because freshness has always been a key success factor to increase sales. The more quickly their products are consumed, the more delicious they taste. Using the SEAM management tools, BPG succeeded in reducing this period to five days in 1985. That success emboldened BPG to imagine alternative organizational and sales strategies to achieve even shorter periods. After five years, BPG achieved and maintained the smallest period possible. Today, when a consumer buys a brioche product in a supermarket, it was probably produced the day before.

The notion of progressively building management capability in this manner is supported by acknowledging the narrow and ultimately useless objective of simply eliminating hidden costs. It is not a practical objective because hidden costs grow back every day and, when viewed from an agility perspective, are useful sources of slack resources. Human behavior, especially the behavior of people who are trying to be better, is not stable. Neither are most internal and external forces. Innovative behaviors and contextual changes create new threats and opportunities and the potential for new dysfunction all the time. Thus, continuously analyzing dysfunctions and converting hidden costs into value-added activity is best thought of as an ongoing business strategy–improvement process. For example, if a strategy depends on product quality, a company may naturally look for hidden costs related to quality defects. Less obvious but equally important, hidden costs may result from "over" quality. In the case of BPG, excess product weight was considered an over-quality hidden cost; it was not a customer requirement and resulted in additional time and raw material costs. Any change in customer requirements increases the likelihood of new hidden costs, even if the internal performance has been stable. So the hidden costs concept must be used over time. It is a strategic analysis concept, not an operational optimization one, and in this sense has little in common with lean management processes.

Similarly, it is nearly impossible to innovate within a highly efficient system. Its shortsighted attention span leaves little room for trials and tests. Experiments, by definition, decrease productivity by pulling resources away from the core task. As a result, hidden costs can be an important source of slack that, when properly acknowledged and focused, become a source of innovation and agility.

Once managers have experienced these processes, an organization's decision-making and operating capabilities tack away from misguided single-loop learning. It leads stakeholders to question the very underpinnings of decision making and helps decision-makers embrace a more nimble, complex, and adaptable way of learning and thinking. It results in a genuine organization-level learning process and transforms organizational patterns from a bureaucratic style into a proactive and agile learning organization.

The Advantages of Patience Over Aggressive Growth

The BPG story clearly demonstrates that developing the ability to make timely, effective, and sustained change is an evolving and emerging capability. Agility is a leadership challenge that is never finished, only approached over time. The story also suggests that consistent above-average profitability is achieved with patience. The lesson for executives in large companies and entrepreneurial start-ups alike is to question and resist the mythology about maximizing profit in the short run or growing aggressively (Stout, 2012). These attitudes support and exacerbate the TFW virus.

Profit maximization and aggressive growth are two of the least examined strategic objectives in organizations. At some level, it is hard to imagine a strategy that is not trying to grow the organization along some dimension: size, profits, revenues, market share, or influence. There is a big difference, however, between aggressiveness that is directed toward taking advantage of a short-term market opportunity and aggressiveness that unceasingly pursues organizational growth rates that greatly exceed the rate of market growth, the market's capacity to sustain growth, or the organization's capacity to support growth.

Aggressive growth hides waste and encourages hidden costs because the speed with which it is pursued and its preeminence as a special situation outside normal systems preclude careful analysis and learning. Too many organizations, especially small, young companies, are encouraged to establish scale and reliability quickly. They are too often encouraged—or maybe better, pressured—to promise stakeholders that they can achieve unreasonable growth or profitability regardless of what is happening to the market for their products and services. However, organizations that embrace the tenets of agility and socio-economic theories are leery of an intent that supports high growth or high returns as a consistent goal. Setting high, difficult-to-achieve, short-term economic goals in service of aggressive growth requires resource allocations that may cause employees to take unreasonable, unethical, or illegal risks to achieve stretch financial goals. The BP/Deepwater Horizon, Enron, and Lehman Brothers scenarios are cautionary tales that still ring in our ears.

Young firms must be more careful about calling for fast growth than other organizations. Their cultures, identities, and brand images are being formed, and the outcomes of this formation have a large effect on the organization's sustained profitability in the future. By the same token, a too narrow focus on maximizing profitability distracts the organization from creating future potential and robs resources that can be applied to social or ecological issues that are central to other aspects of sustainability. The performance records across multiple industries clearly support the conclusion that rapid growth and supra-normal profitability are not sustainable, and executives should view well-publicized exceptions for what they are.

BPG's strategic intents increased in breadth and matured in their differentiators, but they were never overly aggressive. In fact, BPG's international strategy was specifically called out as ambitious in scope and cautious in execution.

One of the benefits of this approach was the emergence of an identity that was not tied to growth. Under the "power of sites, lightness of headquarters" identity, BPG's answer to "who we are" was not defined by "how fast we grow." An identity that reinforces the power of sites over a strong centralized HQ organization encouraged a type of change on the one hand, but did not encourage reckless growth. BPG was wildly successful because it was consistently profitable, not because it was growing wildly. As a result, BPG's identity never revolved around aggressiveness.

From the perspective of other industries, such as fashion retail or high technology, BPG's pace of change was never very high. The BPG case—over forty years of work—was not some mad dash to a finish line. BPG had consistent values around the growth of the business, but over the twenty-seven-year period between 1986 and 2013, its compound annual sales growth was only slightly higher than the growth rate of the overall French economy (for example, compare BPG's 12.3 percent CAGR to France's 10 percent CAGR during the same period, from $758.5 billion in 1986 to $2,735 billion in 2013). It is the "slightly higher" modifier that characterizes agility. Agile organizations are not always the highest performers, but they are usually a little better than average all the time. In this sense, the SEAM approach helped BPG grow without waste. It helped BPG see that efficiency and slack were both important, but different, types of resources. Growth did not have to result in a bloated, inefficient organization. Rather, SEAM helped BPG grow into an efficient and flexible organization.

BPG's measured and patient approach to growth points to the importance of viewing agility as a journey, not a race or destination. More often, growth is a headlong rush of "just do it." For BPG, growth was a consistent pursuit, but it was not an obsessive compulsion. No doubt, viewing agility as a journey and not a destination will be viewed as naïve by some and contrary to today's short-term, winner-take-all, greed grab. Others will see it as a breath of fresh air, confirming a sense that something is deeply wrong with the other perspective and its relationship to TFW virus thinking.

Conclusion

The BPG case describes how young, start-up organizations emerging on the scene today can plan to not only survive but thrive. We believe BPG has become an agile organization and, with continued attention to its identity and the agile routines, it is likely to do better than average over the long run. We have endeavored to paint a picture of how BPG moved from one momentary competitive advantage to the next, guided by conservative financial goals and an identity that helped to achieve both social and economic objectives. BPG embraced change and took risks. More often than not, they were successful. However, BPG mitigated those risks through vigilance processes that kept its fingers on the pulse of near- and long-term issues, an orientation toward trying out new ideas, and an ability to quickly scale up or withdraw from a particular commitment. This does not and should not be construed to mean that agile, socio-economic organizations are perfect. They make mistakes, sometimes large ones. But with the agile routines in place—and one cannot say this about traditional organizations—BPG is more likely to be resilient, to bounce back from a mistake, and to execute changes that bring the organization into profitability more quickly.

A start-up organization can, of course, run the race to scale and reliability, be acquired, and make its founders rich. The allure and pursuit of such a recipe, like the short-sighted devotion to TFW-motivated efficiency, is not likely to fade away any time soon. However, in doing so, both the acquired and the acquirer will have unwittingly perpetuated the TFW virus. The "all or nothing" pace of most start-ups may quickly prove their business concept, but they do so at high hidden costs and with the organization possessing an identity that sees aggressiveness as a key to success. While partly true—aggressiveness did contribute to short-term success—such an identity is not likely to lead to long-term, sustained, and above-average profitability. It will, instead, be a part of a business model that destroys value—rather than creates value—for society. Agile, socio-economic organizations define value differently and in multi-dimensional ways. An alternative path—in our minds a better and more sustainable one—is provided by the BPG example. Really, truly respecting people as valuable, pursuing steady and disciplined growth, and establishing an identity that views change as normal created an agile organization and created social and economic value.

References

Lawler, E. E., III, and Worley, C. (2011). *Management reset.* San Francisco, CA: Jossey-Bass.

Mohrman, S., and Worley, C. (2009). "Dealing with rough times: A capabilities development approach to surviving and thriving." *Human Resource Management, 48*(3), 443–445.

Mohrman, S., and Worley, C. (2010). "The organizational sustainability journey." *Organizational Dynamics, 39*, 289–294.

O'Toole, J., and Bennis, W. (2009). "A culture of candor." *Harvard Business Review*, *87*(6), 54–61.

Stout, L. (2012). *The shareholder value myth: How putting shareholders first harms investors, corporations, and the public.* San Francisco, CA: Berrett-Koehler.

Worley, C., and Lawler, E. E., III. (2009). "Building a change capability at Capital One Financial." *Organizational Dynamics*, *38*(4), 245–251.

Worley, C., Feyerherm, A., and Knudsen, D. (2010). "Building a collaboration capability for sustainability." *Organizational Dynamics*, *39*, 325–334.

About the Authors

CHRISTOPHER G. WORLEY is a professor of strategy and entrepreneurship at the NEOMA Business School in France and strategy director for the Center for Leadership and Effective Organizations (CLEO). He is also a senior research scientist at the Center for Effective Organizations (USC's Marshall School of Business). Prior to these appointments, he was a professor of management in Pepperdine University's Master of Science in Organization (MSOD) program and served as director of that program for eight years. His articles on agility and strategic organization design have appeared in the *Journal of Applied Behavioral Science, Journal of Organization Behavior, Strategy+Business, Sloan Management Review*, and *Organizational Dynamics*. He received the 2012 Douglas McGregor "Best Paper" from the *Journal of Applied Behavioral Science*, the Larry Porter Award from the Organization Development Network in 2011, and the Emerald Publishing Emerati Literary Award for best chapter in 2011. He was awarded the Luckman Distinguished Teaching Fellowship in 1997. He is a former chair of the Academy of Management's Organization Development and Change Division. Dr. Worley received his Ph.D. in strategic management from the University of Southern California, an M.S. in organization development from Pepperdine University, an M.S. from Colorado State University, and a B.S. from Westminster College. He is a member of the Strategic Management Society, the Academy of Management, NTL, and the Organization Development Network.

VÉRONIQUE ZARDET is a professor of management sciences in the EUGINOV department, Institut d'Administration des Entreprises of Lyon Business School, where she is the director of the EUGINOV Center (École Universitaire de Gestion Innovante) and director, along with Professor Henri Savall, the founder, of the ISEOR Research Center. She heads the "Research in Socio-Economic Management" master's program. She holds a Ph.D. in management sciences from the University of Lyon. In 2001, she received, with Henri Savall, the Rossi Award from the Academy of Moral and Political Sciences (Institute of France) for their work on the integration of social variables into business strategies. Her research is focused on strategic change management and the improvement of socio-economic performance in companies and organizations.

MARC BONNET is a professor of management in the EUGINOV department, IAE Lyon Business School, and deputy manager of the ISEOR research center. His research in the field of the socio-economic approach to management, based on the Qualimetrics Intervention-Research methodology, has been mainly carried out in industrial companies. With ISEOR colleagues, he has published articles in journals such as the *Journal of Organizational Change Management, International Journal of Action*

Research, Organization Development Journal, Society and Business Review, and *Organizational Research Methods.*

AMANDINE SAVALL is an intervener-researcher at the IS-EOR research center in Lyon, France, where she has carried out various interventions in European and American companies. She holds a Ph.D. with a concentration in international management and SEAM from Conservatoire National des Arts et Métiers in Paris. She teaches graduate, undergraduate, and doctoral courses at IAE Lyon business school. Her research interests are SEAM, management consulting, management control, family businesses, and international management, using the qualimetrics methodology. In 2014, Amandine was awarded the best doctoral student paper by the Academy of Management's Management Consulting Division. She has coordinated two books edited by Tony Buono and Henri Savall, in the Research in Management Consulting Series, Information Age Publishing.

The Research Sponsor Organizations

The Center for Effective Organizations (CEO)

The Center for Effective Organizations (CEO) is a research center in the Marshall School of Business at the University of Southern California. Founded in 1979, it is the original research center of its kind. CEO's mission is to improve how effectively organizations are managed. It brings together researchers and executives to jointly explore critical organizational issues that involve the design and management of complex organizations. Its leading-edge research in the areas of organizational effectiveness and design has earned it an international reputation for research that influences management practice and makes important contributions to academic research and theory. *Business Week* ranked CEO as one of the top three organizational effectiveness research centers in the United States. *Fortune* magazine recently mentioned CEO as one of the major sources of research information on U.S. industrial competitiveness.

CEO research findings have been published in leading academic journals such as the *Academy of Management Journal*, *Academy of Management Review*, *Harvard Business Review*, *Organizational Dynamics*, *Sloan Management Review*, *Human Relations*, the *Journal of Applied Psychology*, and *The Journal of Applied Behavioral Science*. CEO research findings have been reported and quoted in many leading business and popular publications including *Business Week*, *Fortune*, *Industry Week*, the *Los Angeles Times*, *The New York Times*, *The Wall Street Journal*, and *The Washington Post*.

The Institute for Socio-Economic Organization Research (ISEOR)

The ISEOR research center was created in 1975 by Professor Henri Savall to carry out research on the socio-economic approach to management (SEAM). His seminal book, *Work and People*, first published in French in 1974, explained the need to experiment with the compatibility between social and economic objectives in any kind of organization. It required demonstrating the importance of "hidden costs" and their relationship to performance. Hidden costs are "extra costs," such as overconsumption, and opportunity costs, such as the non-creation of potential. Those costs stem from absenteeism, work accident and occupational diseases, staff turnover, non-quality and productivity gaps. Typical accounting, financial, and information systems overlook these hidden costs and their impact on performance. The SEAM method is taught in many bachelor's, master's, Ph.D., and DBA programs and helps students and executives face the complex and blurry business environment challenges in which they operate.

ISEOR is a self-funded research center and, for more than forty years, ISEOR researchers have carried out intervention-research projects in 1,850 companies and organizations in seventy-two industries across forty countries on four continents. Those organizations include very small businesses and family businesses, as well as multi-national companies, public service organizations, and territories. Overall, 600 researchers have been involved and 140 Ph.D. dissertations have been defended. In addition, forty books and numerous articles have been published and the SEAM methodology has been presented at a variety of academic conferences. The research outcomes and impacts have also been presented in conferences co-sponsored with the Academy of Management, the American Accounting Association, and Instituto Internacional de los Costos.

The Center for Leadership and Effective Organizations (CLEO)

The Center for Leadership and Effective Organizations (CLEO) is the flagship research center at the NEOMA Business School in France. Its mission is to develop, deliver, and share, in the most rigorous and relevant ways possible, the leadership and organizational knowledge that matters most to sustained performance and effectiveness.

As a member of the NEOMA community, CLEO collaborates with executives in France, the EU, and other regions to explore international management issues at the intersection of agility, leadership, collaboration, and sustainability. It offers research, training, and consulting solutions in organization design, leadership development, and change management that address the most pressing complex, strategic, and large-scale challenges. CLEO researchers collaborate with executives to develop and deliver integrated solutions, not just recommendations, that accelerate change, increase leadership capacity, and build robust capabilities. The active involvement of executives as partners creates a learning cycle that helps organizations become adaptable, not just adapt. It is the practical spirit of partnership and collaboration among diverse stakeholders that creates the ability to make timely, effective, and sustained organization change.

CLEO's research is the foundation for its educational and certificate programs. It offers practical, relevant, research-based seminars in collaboration, leadership, agility, organization design, and change management.

Index